272828

NEW HORIZONS OF ECONOMIC PROGRESS

Leo M. Franklin, 1870–1948

NEW HORIZONS OF
ECONOMIC PROGRESS

The Franklin Memorial Lectures
Volume XII

Edited by LAWRENCE H. SELTZER
Holder of the Leo M. Franklin Memorial Lectureship
in Human Relations at
Wayne State University for the year 1961–62

DETROIT—WAYNE STATE UNIVERSITY PRESS—1964

The lectures in this volume were broadcast locally by
WDET (Wayne State University), nationally through the
facilities of the National Association of Educational Broad-
casters, and internationally by the Voice of America.

The Leo M. Franklin Lectures and the Holders of the Leo M. Franklin Memorial Lectureship in Human Relations at Wayne State University

† Out of print.   * To be published in 1965.
Titles of volumes differ in some instances from titles of lectures as originally announced.

Contents

Preface

THE FIVE LECTURES in this volume comprise the twelfth annual Leo M. Franklin Memorial Lectures in Human Relations. They were presented at Wayne State University in the spring of 1962. Minor changes in some of the lectures, mainly to update factual references, were made by the authors in preparing them for publication.

This annual series of lectures was inaugurated by the university in 1950 under a grant from Temple Beth El of Detroit. It was named to honor the memory of the late Dr. Leo M. Franklin, who had been rabbi of Temple Beth El from 1899 to 1941 and Rabbi Emeritus thereafter until his death in 1948; and who, throughout his long and fruitful career, had shown a deep concern with problems of human relations.

Under the terms of the grant, a faculty committee each year recommends to the president of the university a member of the faculty who is to be named the Franklin Memorial Professor for the following year. It becomes his duty to organize and present a series of lectures, by himself and others, dealing with some significant contemporary aspect of human relations. In keeping with my special professional interests, I chose the topic "New Horizons of Economic Progress."

I wish to thank President Clarence B. Hilberry and my other colleagues at Wayne State University for the compliment they paid me in selecting me to be the Franklin

1

Memorial Professor for 1962, and to thank my fellow-lecturers in this series for their ready co-operation and their stimulating contributions.

LAWRENCE H. SELTZER

Introduction

THE GREAT DEPRESSION of the 1930's generated gloomy views of the future in all the Western countries. Unemployment was of massive proportions and appeared to be intractable. In every country, though in varying degree, the cyclical downturn in production and employment was badly aggravated by restrictive governmental and private measures in the fields of monetary, banking, and fiscal policies. These had the effect not only of directly reducing aggregate spending and income, but of causing further shrinkage by intensifying operating losses of business and declines in capital values, and by preventing the public from satisfying its heightened desire for liquidity.

The depression was everywhere intensified by a drastic shrinkage in international trade. Each country sought to reduce its own unemployment by imposing sharper restrictions upon imports from others, with the result that all reciprocally curtailed one another's markets and disrupted established patterns of production and trade.

It is common for men to see the future as an extension of the present. The economic stagnation that came to prevail during the Great Depression was soon rationalized as a chronic tendency of advanced capitalistic societies. The high growth rates of the several preceding centuries (which, however, had also been subject to sharp interruptions) were explained away by attributing them to a fortunate combination of forces which had provided abundant

3

opportunities for the profitable employment of savings and entrepreneurial energies, but which were now believed to be seriously weakened.

First, attention was called to the disappearance of the geographical frontier. Always throughout the preceding centuries there had been vast areas of new territory, such as our own West, to be populated and exploited; now there were few such areas left.

Second, it was observed that the rate of population growth had declined during the decade ended in the mid-thirties; a continuance of this decline was now expected and this expectation led to the prospect of diminishing opportunities for productive investment in housing, industrial and commercial buildings, public utility enterprises, and other segments of the economy.

Third, it was observed that no great new capital-using industries, comparable to the railroads, the telephone systems, electric power, and other public utilities, had appeared for some time. In contrast, it was emphasized that the newer products and industries either required relatively little additional capital or actually diminished the amount needed by displacing products or techniques requiring greater capital.

Fourth, in the face of these prospects for declining rates of growth in the opportunities for profitable investment, it was feared that individuals and business enterprises would continue to strive to save for their private purposes at an undiminished or possibly increased rate, with the result that the effective demand for the current potential output of labor and other productive resources would be chronically inadequate to keep them fully employed. Hence, chronic stagnation.

World War II shattered the immediate applicability of

these fears and doctrines. There was an abrupt transition from glut to scarcity. The demand for labor and other productive resources became limitless; virtually all goods became scarce. In every belligerent country, and even in some of the neutrals, supplies were so short that governments found it necessary to restrict private expenditure for many goods by various forms of direct rationing.

At the end of World War II, after some months of transition, there began a period of rising peacetime economic activity in all the Western countries. In addition to normal needs, there was a vast amount of reconstruction of devastated areas to be accomplished in Europe, and there were accumulated shortages of many kinds to be made up on both sides of the Atlantic. And large underdeveloped areas of the world now sought access to the capital and technologies of the advanced nations.

As civilian output and employment expanded, a new confidence in the future developed. Business enterprises in all the leading countries launched major programs for modernizing and expanding their plants and equipment. At the same time, both public authorities and private firms responded to the widespread and insistent demand for more and newer housing with extensive new construction. The physical scars of the late war disappeared. And as prosperity grew, tariff barriers and quota and exchange restrictions on international trade and payments among the European countries were progressively relaxed, with highly stimulating effects on the volume of international trade. Subject to continued limitations on movements of capital, full interconvertibility on current account of the currencies of the principal West European countries was finally restored.

By the end of the 1950's the economies of all the West

European countries and of the United States, Canada, Latin America, and Japan had reached levels of output and real income far above any previously achieved. With the high confidence generated by prosperity, many persons freely predicted that the coming decade would become the "Soaring Sixties."

But anyone who took the trouble to review the historical record was aware that a ten-year period of continuous movement in either direction was highly unlikely. Superimposed on a long-term upward trend, cyclical fluctuations up and down have been the rule as far back as our records go. The National Bureau of Economic Research has identified twenty-five such business cycles in the United States during the past hundred years, each consisting of a period of expansion and one of contraction. The periods of expansion have averaged thirty months in duration, and those of contraction, nineteen months, though departures from the average durations of both expansions and contractions have been numerous and sometimes wide. Even during the relatively prosperous period since the end of World War II, this country experienced contractions in economic activity in 1948–49, 1953–54, and 1957–58. And the Soaring Sixties began with a fourth postwar contraction which continued throughout 1960 and the first two months of 1961.

In each postwar recession the question was quickly raised whether we had not reached the end of an era of postwar prosperity built upon war-created shortages, and whether, therefore, in the absence of countervailing governmental policies, we should not expect a relapse into something like the economic stagnation that characterized much of the 1930's. But each of the postwar business recessions proved reassuringly mild and short-lived. Nevertheless, concern has continued in some quarters because, among other reasons, the business expansions since the early 1950's have been so restrained as to leave a heavy volume of involuntary unemployment much of the time. Possibly with some help—intentional and otherwise—from monetary and fiscal policies, we seem to have tamed the *expansionary* as well as the recessionary phase of the business cycle. Moreover, some persons have mistrusted the "naturalness" and durability of the relatively elevated average level of economic activity of recent years because of its considerable dependence upon an unprecedentedly large peacetime volume of defense expenditures—a type of outlay that has sometimes been suddenly and drastically curtailed.

To appraise these and similar doubts about the long-range prospects of our economy, it is essential to have in mind the main features of its characteristic behavior in the past and to consider various avenues of major current changes. The historical record discloses, on the one hand, the secular tendency of our economy to irregular alternating periods of expansion and contraction and to occasional episodes of inflation and deep or prolonged depression. On the other hand, it also discloses that our economy is driven by some powerful forces making for economic progress, and that it is capable of great mobility in its use of productive resources.

Thus between 1910 and 1960, the selective breeding of hardier and more productive plants and animals, and the expanded use of fertilizers and machinery, had phenomenal results in agriculture. In 1910 it required 13.6 million farm workers to grow food, fibre, and tobacco for our coun-

try's total population of 92 million; fifty years later it took
only 7 million farm workers to supply a more abundant
satisfaction of these needs for a population grown to 181
million, or about twice as large.[1] Had our productive efficiency in farming remained at the same level as in 1910,
we would have needed something like 50 million farm
workers to produce 1960's agricultural output.[2] Even in the
single decade between 1950 and 1960, farm output per
man-hour in the United States rose by nearly 86 per cent,
and it tripled between 1940 and 1960.[3] It should be noted
that improved technology *off* the farm, as well as on it,
contributed to these increases in agricultural efficiency.
Chemical fertilizers and pesticides, and industrially produced tractors, trucks, and automobiles are examples. Motor vehicles have largely replaced horses and mules on
farms and released the farmland and labor formerly
needed to feed and care for the latter. Factory workers
now do some of the jobs formerly done on farms, such as
preparing livestock feed.

No less striking has been the tenfold increase in our
total yearly manufacturing output between the census of
1899 and 1962, an increase four times as large as the rise
in our population in this period.[4] Contributing to the dis-
proportionate gain in industrial output were the rising
levels of education and skills in our working population
and the ever-increasing and more efficient investment in
plants and equipment. The gains in agricultural and industrial efficiency, supplemented by a large increase in the
employment and output of the service trades and professions, enabled us to raise the average standard of living in
this country to a level never before attained anywhere.

These impressive advances in the conquest of poverty

during the last two generations have been accompanied by an enormous reduction in painful toil for most workers in mines, factories, construction projects, and homes—no less a boon because it does not lend itself readily to measurement.

Can we reasonably look forward to further great advances in economic well-being? Without attempting a coordinated examination of all the possibilities, four professional economists and a labor leader examine in the following essays five horizons on which such progress may well take place. One of them reviews some of the main monetary and fiscal problems of our contemporary economy, and points to flexible measures that may be used to restrain cost-push inflation when employment is high, and mass loss of jobs when a business recession threatens. Another discusses the possible use of various governmental policies to reduce the wastage of both manpower and material resources that results from interruptions and reversals of economic growth. A third analyzes the important economic effects of rapidly cumulating additions to our knowledge and skills—immaterial capital that is even more important than factory buildings and machines in promoting economic progress. A fourth discusses the shortcomings and possibilities of our educational institutions as instruments of economic progress. The fifth and last deals with the emergence of the Common Market and its relation to the prospects and benefits of a large expansion of international trade.

L. H. S.

I
Problems of the American Economy— Hard and Easy

by
PAUL A. SAMUELSON

PAUL A. SAMUELSON, Ph.D., president of the
American Economic Association in 1961, and an economic
adviser to the late President John F. Kennedy, is an economist with a worldwide reputation. Born in Gary, Indi-
ana, he was educated at the University of Chicago and
Harvard University, and has been professor of economics
at Massachusetts Institute of Technology since 1940. He
is the author of the most widely used college textbook in
economics ever published, a work that has been translated
into a dozen foreign languages. He has made brilliant
contributions to his field and has served as a consultant
to various agencies of the federal government.

Problems of the American Economy—Hard and Easy *

WITH SOME TREPIDATION I undertook to prepare a
Franklin Lecture on certain new-fashioned principles of
modern economics, being acutely aware that much of what
I say will sound opposed to old-fangled principles of economics we associate with Benjamin Franklin's *Poor Rich-
ard's Almanac.* I found it heartening therefore to learn
that Dr. Leo M. Franklin was himself a pioneer in social
and humanitarian movements. And upon reflection, I realized that it is a libel on the memory of that versatile
scientist to think that Benjamin Franklin was a staid dog-
matist on economic matters: For it was Franklin who
espoused a regime of paper money in the Pennsylvania
colony; not, as skeptics think, because he was a printer but
rather because the actual experience of Pennsylvania
showed that it enjoyed one of the longest periods of prosperity under such a regime of money management to be
found in the early American annals.

Not long ago I was invited to give a public lecture in
England, and sat down to write out some of the things
American economists worry about. You may be sure the
list was not a short one. Ours may in some sense be an affluent society, but the day in which all economic problems
wither away is still far off in the future. There is nothing

* Although this was delivered before President Kennedy's death, sub-
sequent events and the Kennedy-Johnson 1964 tax cut seem to corroborate
its general viewpoint.

13

surprising in what I have said yet. But the order of importance which I will attach to the different economic problems might seem very surprising to a non-economist. For example, if you go to a good businessman's club or if you listen to heated political debates on radio and television, you might be forgiven for thinking that one of the most important economic problems facing America today is that of the outstanding public debt and the rate at which it is growing as a result of deficit fiscal policies. Now I would be among the first to recognize that there are some geniune economic problems connected with the level of our outstanding public debt; yet in all candor I must admit that the debt would not appear in the first half dozen problems that most concern an expert in political economy today. How we deploy our economic resources to enhance the security of America and the free world in these cold war days is a tremendously more important problem than that of the debt. Our international balance of payments is a much more important problem. Our past and future growth rate is more important. Unemployment is more important. So, I think, is the problem of urban blight and regional development.

I could go on listing problems indefinitely. Still one thing that we economists are supposed to believe in is the division of labor, and perhaps not everyone should worry about everything. This was brought home to me some considerable years ago when I gave a luncheon address to the austere Boston Finance Club. In the course of my talk some reference was made to the problem of gold, which I could see was beginning to rear its ugly head again. After thanking me prettily for my speech, the master of ceremonies said: "I was specially struck by your remarks about gold, particularly when I realized that I haven't heard the subject mentioned since way back in the 1930's. At that time everybody seemed to talk about nothing else. How I used to worry about the problem! Until finally one morning I pulled myself together and made a firm resolution. 'I have too many things to worry about already. From now on I'm going to let somebody else worry about gold.' And you know I've been a happy man ever since." Well, since 1957 gold has become more of a problem and there are fewer happy men these days.

Of course the good Lord did not create the world so as to make economists happy. It would be irresponsible of me, just in order to attain extra peace of mind, to stick my head in the ground and ignore a problem. I am afraid, though, some ivory tower economists are a bit like that. For example, last academic year we had one of America's most brilliant theorists as a visiting professor at Massachusetts Institute of Technology. You may recall that late in October at the height of the 1960 Presidential campaign there was something of a gold crisis in the London market. Speculators were so avid to hoard gold that they bid the price from its normal level of about $35 an ounce up to $40 an ounce or more. Some of us economists were sitting around the lunch table discussing the matter. When I expressed my concern, our brilliant visiting professor said: "Stop worrying about the gold problem." Most of us were amazed to hear our guest telling us he was not particularly worried about the gold drain. Finally our chairman had the wit to ask: "Adam Smith,"—I must confess that I disguise the name to protect the guilty—"what is it that you do worry about?" The answer was informative: "Why should I worry about gold? I don't worry about anything!"

15

That may be an admissible attitude for someone in the ivory tower to take; but any economist who sticks his neck out of the ivory tower must pursue another strategy. As President Truman once said: "If you can't stand the heat, stay out of the kitchen." In my youth there used to be in gift shops something called a *worry bird*. You bought this little wooden artifact for a few dollars and then turned all your worries over to it. I am afraid that we economists who address ourselves to policy problems have to be on the firing line; we cannot buy draftees to keep us out of the army. It is our job to be the worry birds for the nation; that's what we get paid for. When my descendants gather about my knee and say, "Grandpa, what did you do to add to the gross national product?" my reply will have to be, "I worried."

Hard Problems

Let me now list a few economic problems, roughly in order of their importance, first giving the intrinsically hard ones and second those that are in a certain sense easy.

1. *The problem of excessive unemployment.* The percentage of people unable to find work has grown at each business cycle peak during the last decade. Although the first year and a half of the Kennedy recovery reduced unemployment from 7 per cent of the civilian labor force to 5½ per cent, we never came near the 2½ per cent level of a decade ago. And even the minimal 4 per cent proximate goal never came clearly in sight. Few countries in the Western world have had so poor a record as ours, and I say this even after making the necessary adjustments for the lack of comparability between our statistical measuring rods and theirs.

2. *The problem of creeping cost-push inflation.* For most of this century the cost of living has shown a persistent upward trend. What has become most disquieting is the apparent recent tendency for prices and wages to rise even when America is still intolerably far from reasonably full employment and capacity production.

3. *The problem of our chronic international balance-of-payments deficit.* At first in the postwar years, there was a tendency for us to sell more abroad than foreigners could pay for by sending us their goods. All this changed in the last decade; and our private exports of goods and services no longer exceed private imports by an amount sufficient to enable us to carry on (1) our public, military, and civilian aid programs and (2) our private long-term investments abroad. The result has been a steady drain of our gold supply, a steady piling up of short-term IOU's to the rest of the world, and a shakier confidence in the stability of the dollar.

4. *The problem of growth in our full-employment potential to produce.* West Germany, Japan, France, Italy, and the Netherlands—to say nothing of the collectivistic Soviet Union—have been demonstrating postwar growth rates far above our postwar average. How can a mixed economy, dominated by private initiative but subject to public control and stimulus, raise its average rate of growth from, say, $3\frac{1}{2}$ per cent to $4\frac{1}{2}$ or 5 per cent?

All these are hard economic problems, and important ones.

"Easy" Economic Problems

1. *The problem of federal deficits and rising public debt.* The 1950's and early 1960's look to be years of al-

most continuous unbalance in the budget (the so-called Administrative Budget).

2. *The problem of automation.* It is widely believed that we have now moved into a second industrial revolution, in which computers, servo-mechanisms, and robots will make man technologically obsolete, causing mass unemployment and necessitating a drastic shortening of the work week.

3. *The problem of disarmament's economic impact.* Were peace to "break out," would mass unemployment and chronic slump like that of the 1930's be the inevitable fate of the American economy, showing that our vaunted postwar prosperity depends necessarily on armament expenditure?

4. *The problem of our inability to forecast the future.* If we cannot decide what conditions will be later, how can we now initiate the proper economic programs?

"These are easy problems?" you will ask. "If automation and sudden end of the cold war are easy, then heaven defend us from the hard ones."

In reply, let me clarify the sense in which such problems can be classified as easy. Provided that we learn how to solve the hard problems in the first list, the secondary problems can have a straight-forward solution. It is in this sense that they may be called easy.

Ideology as a Debit [1]

A problem like that of the public debt becomes major because of its psychological rather than economic nature, as the following will show.

Back in January, 1961, my task force made a report to

President-elect Kennedy on the American economy (January 4, 1961). The general pattern envisaged in it turned out, by some sad miracle, to have been right:

(i) the thing to fear was not the persistence of the 1960 recession itself, but rather the danger that the next recovery would be a disappointing one like that of 1959–60;

(ii) unemployment looked to remain a problem well into the new recovery;

(iii) the American economy appeared to need nothing so much as a *stimulus in its over-all demand spending,* such as a vigorously expansionary monetary policy and *a planned* ("prudent") *deficit* could alone give it.

In pointedly opposing the Eisenhower philosophy of contained government expenditures and "sound" budget balance (like that appropriate to any civilian or army family), I was merely reflecting the considered opinions of the bulk of economists who have been analyzing the facts about national income determination and American growth. While these are the views that scholars all over the free world are almost unanimous in holding, they have never been the views of the man in the street. And in Congress itself the Eisenhower philosophy, as interpreted by Secretary George Humphrey (in opposition to the then Economic Advisor Arthur F. Burns) and by Secretary Anderson (in opposition to no heard voice in the last Eisenhower administration), had led to a *reversion* of economic understanding even among the moderate leadership of the Democrats—as exemplified by such men as Vice-President Johnson and the late Congressman Rayburn. Needless to say the Byrds and Goldwaters in Congress required no Eisenhower influence to make them revert to a position they had never left.

I linger on this irrational question of ideology because it must have made the job of the new Administration a hard one. Had President Kennedy come out boldly for the sizable deficit which objective economic analysis called for, he would have run into severe opposition in the divided Congress; and, by becoming tarred with the asinine label of an "irresponsible spender," the President might have put all his new programs in jeopardy. Here then was one of those reminders that politics is the art of the feasible: while it is always easy for expert advisers to urge that the head of state exercise his "leadership," he must ever deliberate on how best to spend and conserve his limited bank-balance of leadership.

Though the outgoing Administration bequeathed a budget document purporting to show a budget in balance, it was readily apparent to any intelligent observer that it was bequeathing an economy which was already running a deficit and which could not possibly end up the fiscal year without a still bigger one. The fact that the deficit could be blamed on the previous Administration eased the ideological task; and in the early messages, President Kennedy described his own program as one of "balancing the Eisenhower Budget," in the sense of recommending programs that would not of themselves unbalance the budget if it had been true that the Eisenhower Budget had been itself in balance—which, because of the decline in tax revenues due to the recession, it clearly was not. (If the above sentence is an involved one, no blame attaches to me as a writer but must instead be attributed to the subtlety of its content.)

Bluntly, the straight economics of the 1961 situation required a sizable deficit. How might this best come about?

There were a number of new Kennedy programs that could be justified on their intrinsic merits, independently of any anti-recession need. A temporary tax cut, with or without some relinquishing by Congress of discretionary authority, was a possibility. Structural improvements in our unemployment compensation system and in other transfer programs naturally recommended themselves. On the other hand, the outlook for defense expenditures at the beginning of 1961 was cloudy, and expert opinion could be found suggesting that these would not have to rise in any appreciable amount.

Whatever the economic merits of a tax cut, this was then politically out of the question. The President had run on a platform that asked sacrifices of the American people. How then could he begin by giving them what many would regard as a "handout?" Also, how could one be sure that the new civilian and defense programs might not require maintenance of the tax base? And what about the possibility of raising our growth rate by changing our full-employment composition of demand away from consumption and toward net capital formation by means of maintaining tax rates and offsetting the ultimate implied full-employment budget surplus by a militant policy of credit expansion?

In the first years of this recovery there has not seemed to be much steam behind the American economy. Car sales and residential contracts have been the only bright spots. Business investment in equipment and stocks has simply not been buoyant. The verdict seems to be increasingly evident that this recovery has been one primarily dependent upon government stimulus. If it were somehow possible to divide up the total forces making for expansion into the

21

mutually exclusive categories of private and public, I suspect that the contribution of the private sector would compare unfavorably with that of most historical recoveries.

I state this as a fact, not as an accusation. I do not think it is really anybody's fault. With the war seventeen years behind us and in the face of the comfortable levels of capacity relative to effective dollar demand, I would find it rather rational were I a businessman to be behaving about as they have generally been doing. A corollary of this view, that capitalists cannot be charged with being on a deliberate sit-down strike, is this: the undoubted friction which has grown up between President Kennedy and the business community cannot validly be given much blame for the lack of steam in the American economy.

Since 1956 economists have become increasingly suspicious that we are in an intermediate period where the only thing that can bring the American economy close to a full employment growth rate is an unusually expansionary fiscal and monetary policy. With the international balance of payments putting a constraint upon militant use of stimulating credit policy, the burden cannot help but be put upon fiscal policy. This means, let us face it, a sizable deficit in what is called the Administrative Budget.

As one of our leading economists said privately, "It may be that the optimal deficit of the United States in the next few years is about equal to our so-called largest peacetime deficit, the unplanned $12 billion of President Eisenhower in fiscal 1959." Should this diagnosis turn out to be at all near the mark, the prospect would not be too cheerful. For there is little evidence as yet that many of our congressmen and voters have been able to overcome their ideological opposition to large government deficits.

A Basic Cost-Push Problem?

After these preliminaries, let me state bluntly what it is that I do worry about. I am fearful that *the institutions of our American economy are such that any time we approach reasonably close to full employment, we thereby face the threat of an inflationary price creep*. Such an inflationary price increase has repercussions on the distribution of income between old and young, between creditors and debtors. It has repercussions on the deterioration of our international balance of payments. It jeopardizes the successful attainment of high levels of employment and the banishment of unemployment. It increases the political pressures for restrictive tariff barriers and for other costly devices (such as lowering the length of the working week to far below what workers would really want if given the choice of steady employment). And, of course, as a result of all this, it threatens to hamper seriously our rate of growth —in comparison with that of the Soviet Union or other parts of the world.

The problem I speak of is by no means peculiar to the United States. If you read English books and newspapers, you will note much concern there over the possibility of a cost-price spiral. The same seems to be true of Sweden and the other Scandinavian countries. I wish I knew the underlying reasons why West Germany, and perhaps Japan, do not seem to be susceptible to this modern ailment in so great a degree as is the United States. (The Soviet Union and the totalitarian economies on the other side of the Iron Curtain are not immune from all economic problems. Russia in the past had terrible famines and Mainland

China may right now be suffering from similar catastrophes. A change in the pace of industrialization for military expenditure must cause massive reallocations of labor even in planned economies. The USSR has had to rely for years on heavy turnover taxes to keep down the excess of consumer purchasing power. But so long as a centralized governmental authority can put controls on wages and prices by direct fiat, the problem is a different one from that I am describing for the Western democracies.)

I do not wish to sound dogmatic. My diagnosis may be a false one and I may be a doctor in search of a disease that isn't there. It would delight me immensely if I turned out to be wrong and there proved not to be in the American economy any basic tendency toward "cost-push" or "sellers' inflation." I cheerfully admit that a minority of modern economists, including some very good ones, believe that cost-push inflation is a mirage and an illusion.

The Perfectly-Competitive Artificial Model

How can we best understand the mechanism of cost-push inflation? I think it will be useful to start out by mentioning a quite artificial economic model in which all wages and prices are determined in *perfectly*-competitive markets. Just imagine that all consumers goods were to be auctioned off for what they would bring, in the way that wheat is auctioned off on the floor of the Board of Trade in Chicago. Since we know that in the real world goods are predominantly sold by manufacturers and retailers who name a price and then wait for the consumer to decide how much he will buy at that price, this notion of an auctioneer's market requires some stretch of the imagination.

But I must ask you to stretch your imaginations still further. Imagine that labor too is auctioned off. I don't have in mind the slavery markets of Charleston and Savannah; but I do picture a model in which each day or each month we all throw our labor services on the market to fetch whatever wage rate will be determined by spirited supply and demand offerings and biddings. Unless I am an utterly useless person, possessing ten thumbs and being a trouble-maker to boot, I need never in such a world be unemployed. All I have to do is offer to undercut the wage of those now holding jobs, and at the right wage rate I will find employment of some kind. That doesn't mean I can be sure of getting a job with the New York Yankees, or that I can become the Archbishop of Canterbury just by offering to take the job for less. But it does mean that somebody may be able to bump me from my chair of political economy at M.I.T., if he can deliver equally good lectures and is willing to work for less.

Can such an artificial economy as I have described ever experience inflation? Of course it can. Let the Federal Reserve System or the Treasury start printing $100 bills in unlimited amount, spending them on elaborate post offices and battleships, or mailing them to all beyond the retirement age as weekly pensions. There will soon result the classical case of "too much money-spending chasing too few goods." To be sure, if the economy had earlier been experiencing a good deal of unemployment for some unexplained reason, the printing of the new money might *at the very first* cause an expansion of total production. So long as extra employment makes possible a production of new physical goods apace with the creation of money, there would be no need for the price level to rise. But we all realize that there is a limit to total employment and capacity; and after this limit had been reached, further putting out of money from the printing presses would cease to have what the textbooks describe as its "real multiplier effects" and will begin to have "purely price tag multiplier effects."

You will recognize that what I have been talking about is not complete fantasy. Plenty of times in the past, galloping inflations have taken place just along the lines of the model I have been describing. Our own Revolutionary War was an instance and gave rise to the expression "not worth a continental," the latter being the name then given to the printed currency. The same thing happened in the Confederate South during our Civil War. After World War I, the galloping German inflation resulted from unbounded issue of German marks. There are many other examples; and even though our model is an artificial one, it is a pretty good bet that the same thing would happen in modern America if an unlimited amount of money were to be issued by our central bank or Treasury.

What I have been describing would go under the name of "demand-pull" inflation. The image is this: the vast increase of dollar spending pulls up prices. No doubt wages and other costs will rise too, but they would be rising from the indirect pull on prices.[2]

Up until now all my examples of my demand-pull inflation for our ideally competitive economic model have had to do with the creation of currency. Of course, you will realize that operations that are designed to increase the amount of checkable demand deposits can also be construed as effective measures for changing the amount of total money and thereby having repercussions upon price levels. Nor is that all. Governmental fiscal policy can also, in such a model, create changes in the general level of prices. For example, if the government spends much more than it is taxing and finances the difference by means of bond sales to the public, that process too can create an inflationary gap and cause the general price level to rise. If, on the other hand, the government is running a budgetary surplus rather than deficit, the current rate of such a surplus can have a depressing effect upon the price level even prior to any changes in the supply of money or in the long-run level of public debt outstanding.

These various matters can be described in more than one way. Older economists who are fond of terminology like that of the quantity theory of money will say that changes in the velocity of circulation of money can have effects upon total spending and prices just as changes in the total amount of money itself. Economists who like to use the terminology of modern income determination will put the same matter something like this: Changes in government fiscal policy, like changes in central bank policy or in the rate at which mines are turning out gold, will shift the point of intersection of the saving and investment schedules (or of the $C + I + G$ and 45°-line schedules); this can lead to an opening up of the inflationary gap and a resulting demand-pull inflation.

If demand-pull inflation were all we had to fear, life would be simple. It would then be merely a problem of the proper dosage of fiscal and monetary measures: not too much so as to cause inflation; not too little so as to cause excessive unemployment. Thus, when automation had created temporary unemployment, that could be offset by expansionary demand policies; when automation had created over-full-employment, the reverse dosage would be called for. But with wage and other cost inflexibilities, this problem—and others, such as the balance of international payments—may become very hard.

Armaments and Prosperity

"Does America's prosperity depend upon military expenditures? If there were a relaxation of cold war tension and a massive reduction in governmental security expenditures, would the effect on the American economy be a profound crisis, followed by a sustained slump like that of the post-1929 Great Depression?"

When I lecture abroad in Japan or Europe, somebody always eagerly asks these questions. Curiously, American audiences seem less concerned with such issues. Psychoanalysts of businessmen's wives report that their patients' spouses worry about many things, but not over the breaking out of peace.

While the layman in Europe still registers concern that disarmament might cause a capitalistic collapse, there seems to be a new look in Soviet opinion on this matter. The Soviet economic journals, I am told, increasingly take the line that the American economy could weather (and benefit from) extensive demilitarization. Just the year-before-last a group of eminent Soviet economists visited this country to meet with American academicians for an informal and scientific exchange of viewpoints. When they met in Cambridge, Massachusetts, with some of my colleagues at M.I.T. and Harvard University, I was interested to hear that they were prepared to stipulate in advance of the discussion that cessation of the cold war would not engender colossal unemployment and crisis in the United States. Since this was billed as a scientific discussion and not a political free-for-all, I was prepared to believe that their detailed analyses of postwar economic developments in America had led them to reverse the usual Marxian analysis of our problems. I must confess, though, that I did not hear there the scientific reasons for this revisionist attitude.

I am not a Marxian economist. Some years ago Paul Sweezy claimed you could count the Marxian economists in American universities on one nose—his; and it may be significant that he no longer holds a regular university post and the nose is now worn by Stanford's Paul Baran. I am inclined to agree with the recent statement of Peter Wiles, formerly of Oxford and now of Brandeis University, that, although one can detect some influence of bourgeois economics on Soviet practice in the realm of linear programming and input-output, there appears to be no detectable reverse influence of Marxian economics on present-day Anglo-Saxon economics, as she is taught in our institutions of higher learning and as practiced by economic specialists in business and government.

My own preoccupation is with the understanding of behavior in mixed-economies of the American and Western European type. If it is necessary to learn mathematics to help explain them, I steel myself to this task. If it were necessary to learn Sanskrit, I would grudgingly do so. If to predict the pattern of future events an economist had to spend his middle years hanging by his heels from the ceiling, I would perforce make the sacrifice. And if my reading of Marxian economists generated fruitful hypotheses concerning realistic economic behavior, I would unhesitatingly put in the effort. My only sticking point would come if Dr. Faust's devil required my immortal soul in exchange for understanding of political economy; and even here, so great is my zeal for scientific objectivity, I would certainly feel tempted.

An uncommitted student will, I fear, find little to help him in his understanding of the postwar American economy from trying to master the dialectic and language of Marxist economists. In a way I regret this, for our knowledge is not so perfect as to permit us the luxury of spurning help from any source. In other moods when my scientific spirit flickers and the winds of chauvinism sweep through my drowsy thoughts, I find myself enjoying a secret satisfaction that our rivals in the struggle for coexistence should be so weak in their analysis of our system. I suppose this is merely a natural weakness of the flesh and an atavistic survival of the caveman's feeling that for someone to know his name and understand him represents a vague threat to his well-being. Seriously, were I the all-powerful head of a Communist state, I would follow the practice of the ruthless Nazis who created the rank of "honorary" Aryan for those individuals whose scientific or other talents were deemed useful for the Fatherland. That is, I would set up in the Kremlin a secret economic unit, forbidden to hamper itself by the use of Marxian categories, and required to use the most up-to-date of modern economics to analyze Western reality. (I reject as frivolous the view that the best Soviet economists, after they have applied the most powerful M.I.T. methods to analyzing America, then interline their reports with harmless and irrelevant Leninist slogans as a cover.) If, as some wit has said, Marxism is the opiate of the Marxists, there is no reason why the Soviet struggle for dominance should be sacrificed to this luxury activity. I wish to add that my remarks about the sterility of Marxism apply to the understanding of economic trends. Some wiser men than I claim to find benefit from Marxian hypotheses in understanding *political* developments.

A Dollar Is a Dollar Is a Dollar

So much then for Marxian economics in the present context. Nonetheless the questions about the effect of defense expenditures upon the American economy are valid. And they are important. They deserve objective examination and require from us the most careful analysis modern economics can bring to them.

Present-day analysis of income determination makes it quite evident that the additional military expenditures resulting from the Berlin crisis are one of the causes for our vigorous post-recession expansion.

Chairman Heller and his associates on the Council of Economic Advisers were rightly impressed with the size of the gap between our recent performance and our economic potential. They rightly were concerned with the prospect that unemployment would recede slowly; the new facts becoming available are beginning to confirm the Heller view that *the intensification of our unemployment* cannot be attributed primarily to an increase in structural or hard-core unemployment among the aged, young, regionally stranded, and technologically obsolete workers.

From public utterances and published gossip, one infers that the Council of Economic Advisers—taking full

31

account of our international balance of payments position and the risks with respect to creeping inflation of the cost-push type—believed that our economy was in need of more expansionary fiscal monetary policy than appeared politically in the cards a few months ago. It appears to me that the Berlin crisis has fortuitously brought the economy the extra expenditures we needed for a more vigorous recovery. While it reflects a naïve misunderstanding of purchasing-power mechanics to think that military dollars have some extra potency in reviving a capitalistic system and to think that ordinary civilian expenditures and tax cuts could not provide an efficacious substitute, there is no reason to blink the fact that these extra expenditures will be a stimulus in the quarters ahead.

This has a bearing on recent American debates. In April, 1961, Arthur F. Burns, Eisenhower's first Economic Adviser, stated the view that full employment (as defined, for example, by a 4 per cent unemployment rate) would be reached in about the third quarter of 1962. In the August, 1961, *Morgan Guaranty Survey,* Dr. Burns pushed the date for our having come close to full employment to nearer the end of 1962. If Burns was then more nearly correct in his view than the less optimistic Council predictions of the same dates, the addition of the substantial post-Berlin and other new expenditure programs would, one supposes, push the date of 4 per cent unemployment toward the middle of 1962 (or in terms of some of the quantitative expenditure estimates, even earlier still). Now, I find the odds to be against this possibility and to be closer to the Council position when that position is adjusted for the additional programs. But Burns has often been right in the past and may well be vindicated by events. In any case, a person who thinks the Kennedy programs excessive might, even in the face of disappointing unemployment percentages in 1962, shift over to the quite different argument that the very failure of the economy to get down to 4 per cent unemployment would itself suggest that 4 per cent is too "activistic" a definition of present-day full employment. At least this is a view of a colleague, who disagrees with Burns's prediction, but has subscribed all along to the view that *whatever* the Kennedy administration has planned in the way of expenditure expansion has always been too great.

The last four years of the Eisenhower administration did, as I hinted earlier, serve to set back public and congressional understanding concerning rational fiscal policy. That being the case there may well be something to the following argument:

> Proper civilian fiscal and monetary policy are capable of generating enough dollar demand to banish slackness in our economy. True. Yet such may be the state of economic understanding and political ideology as to make it much easier for the American governmental system to do, *in the form of defense and security programs,* the things necessary for high employment.

This hypothesis has nothing to do with the peculiar terminology and models of Marxism, but to the degree that it represents a one-half truth or a three-quarters truth we should recognize it on its own merits.

Before World War II Harvard's Alvin Hansen promulgated the hypothesis of "secular stagnation." By this he meant the natural forces of consumption and investment spending were unlikely to be strong enough to keep us in high employment. He rested his theory on many factors that need not be discussed here.

Postwar employment has been generally high and therefore some would construe this to be a refutation of the Hansen theory. (I imagine that Professor Hansen would today admit that such a reversal of his non-economic expectation as the postwar surge in population has indeed altered his envisaged economic pattern. But certainly he can offer the defense that the population revolution gave no foreshadowing of itself in the prewar vital statistics, and that his critics at the time did not base their case so much on an hypothetical upsurge in population as on the allegation that population trends were not important causal factors in determining the sufficiency of total effective demand.) Hansen can very well argue, and I believe he may somewhere have done so, that it is precisely the increased role of government expenditure that staved off the slackness he feared; and that far from being the boy who cried wolf when there was no wolf, he was the boy who scared off the wolf by crying wolf.

Although Hansen was my revered teacher and is my good friend, I have no vested interest in the stagnationist hypothesis. What I merely want to emphasize here is that the increase in government expenditure, even if balanced by higher tax rates, could achieve whatever favorable effects it was capable of just as much if spent on useful public goods as on useful or useless *arms* programs.

A corollary of the above facts and reasonings appears to me to be this:

A sharp reduction of military expenditures, unlikely as that must seem to a dispassionate observer of world events, would have as its *short-term* consequences a considerable unsettling of production and occupation.

Such transitional difficulties would be minor were one assured that a new configuration of high employment lay just ahead. And, if a sizable reduction in military expenditure were to be followed by considerable tax reduction and by some compensating increase in useful civilian public programs, that would go a long way to offset the deflationary impact of total disarmament.

Nonetheless, in estimating the new configuration of fiscal and monetary policy that would restore high employment, an objective modern economist would have to admit the possibility (1) *that a vigorously expansionary monetary policy would be in order and* (2) *that a prudent budgetary* DEFICIT *would be called for.*

What is the political feasibility that the American people would cheerfully legislate the required budgetary deficit?

This is a question that takes me outside the sphere of my professional economic accomplishments. Still I am willing to venture a tentative guess.

The political pressures in our democracy would, I suspect, become strong to produce whatever deficits are needed to keep unemployment from rising much above say 8 per cent in any brief period. There is no guarantee, though, that those pressures would be efficacious to create whatever deficit is needed to keep unemployment at the 4 per cent level. Moreover, without the dynamic leadership of somebody with the personal magnetism of John F. Kennedy, there would be a significant possibility that our percentage of unemployment could slowly rise and level off at what most of us would regard as a socially undesirable rate.

I do not wish to end upon a pessimistic note. I am quite confident that the American electorate will rise to the future challenges put on it. My reason for discussing the matter is to illustrate the need for an economist who professes to be a scientist to follow his objective analysis wherever it leads him. It is a final bit of irony that Marxists, hypnotized by terminology that may have lacked relevance in its own day and certainly is misleading in the middle of the twentieth century, should still be obsessed by the specter of dramatic capitalistic crisis like that of the 1929 stock market crash rather than appreciating the more realistic Achilles heel of a contemporary mixed economy.

II

Priorities for Freedom's Survival

by
WALTER P. REUTHER

WALTER P. REUTHER, LL.D., president of the UAW-CIO, was born in Wheeling, West Virginia, the son of a labor leader. He attended Wayne State University for three years while working nights in automobile factories. He early became active in organizing automobile workers and has been president of the UAW since 1946, and of the CIO since 1952, as well as a vice-president of the AFL-CIO since its organization in 1955. A man of great energy and strong opinions on controversial issues, he has thrown himself energetically into many social and political causes. Both Wayne State University and the University of Michigan, among other institutions, have awarded him honorary degrees.

Priorities for Freedom's Survival

RABBI FRANKLIN, one of the great spiritual leaders in Detroit when I first came to this city in 1927, would certainly have agreed with the late Rev. A. Powell-Davies, who stated in one of his last sermons: "The world is too dangerous for anything but the truth and too small for anything but brotherhood."

That was and is the truth. The whole world is mined today with the possibility of total destruction in a nuclear holocaust. Yet at the same time there are opportunities for human progress and fulfilment undreamed of in any other period.

The same science and technology which made the H-bomb and intercontinental missile possible have enabled us to create the tools for achieving unprecedented economic abundance; have given us the technical means to satisfy man's fundamental economic and material needs.

For the first time in the history of the human family, we are within reach of mastering our physical environment if—and this is the crucial condition—if we can prevent a nuclear war and lay the foundations of a world community in which all people can reach out and share in the fruits of freedom and advancing technology.

We come back, then, to the insight of A. Powell-Davies: the understanding that the crisis of the world is not essentially economic, political, or military in character, but moral.

Put in other terms, we are the creators and the victims of a grave cultural lag between growing technical and scientific proficiency on the one hand and, on the other, lagging moral wisdom and social intelligence. Progress in the physical mastery of nature has outrun man's capacity to master himself. Achievement in the natural sciences has been more considerable than our education in the skills and arts of living together on a planet where distances between different countries and different people are diminishing.

Failure to close this gap between knowledge and wisdom has put peace and freedom in jeopardy; has made the guided missile available to misguided men.

We meet at a time when the nations are once more trying to reach accords leading to disarmament. Whatever the results of a particular conference, we must press constantly for agreements that will lift from mankind the tremendous economic burden—and the tremendous risk —of the arms race. Peace in the age of the H-bomb and the ballistic missile has indeed become the indispensable condition for human survival.

General Medaris, former chief of the army missile program, told an AFL-CIO conference on world affairs not very long ago that this country's nuclear capability, without any additions to our arsenal, has a destructive power equivalent to ten tons of TNT for every man, woman and child in the world. And the Russians have a roughly comparable potential.

The security inherent in this superabundance of overkill is highly precarious. The human family must put an end to the nuclear arms race or the nuclear arms race will put an end to the human race.

We shall not find a way out of this dilemma simply or quickly. We cannot, given the nature of the world we have created and must live in, simply drop our guard against aggression. Yet we must begin to *turn* toward peace.

We must, that is, act in the knowledge that military power is but the negative aspect of the total effort we must make if peace and freedom are to be made secure in this troubled and complicated world.

Our destructive capabilities are awesome. Yet they are a wasting asset. If we are to win through to a real peace we must augment freedom's positive capability. The ultimate challenge to communism lies not in democracy's destructive stockpile but in its creative energies and intelligence.

There is a vast field for the exercise of those energies and that intelligence. Yet there is no enterprise more desperately in need of their exercise than that of bringing our great human and natural resources to bear in lessening and eventually eliminating the economic and social disparities that separate the highly developed from the underdeveloped countries.

There are really two cold wars rather than one. The confrontation of Western and Soviet power in the heartland of Europe might be likened to the relatively static war of attrition that began in 1914 when the Germans were stopped at the Marne.

Then there is what might be called the cold war of movement swirling in Latin America, Africa, and Asia and intimately bound up with the revolution of discontent and rising expectations sweeping those other continents.

The confrontation in Europe is really a holding action. The shape of the future may well be determined by the boldness, imagination, and compassion we bring to the contest for the hearts and minds of the millions who live in the emerging nations. It is here in the have-not lands that democracy can go over to the offensive by enabling the two-thirds of humanity who today live at or below the subsistence level to enter the economic world of the mid-twentieth century.

We should not pay communism the compliment of believing that the Kremlin started the revolution now sweeping Asia, Africa, and much of Latin America. We must see it rather as a Western legacy; the genie in the lamp was not Marx or Lenin, but Sam Adams and Tom Paine, Thomas Jefferson and the men who stormed the Bastille. The revolution of rising expectations in our time was born out of the explosive mixture of the Declaration of Independence and Western technology. It began in 1776, not 1917.

Technologically, the world has become a neighborhood. And this neighborhood has caught fire with the idea that "all men are created equal." Poverty, hunger, ignorance, and disease still scourge the have-not lands, yet they have been rejected in the minds of their victims. The most illiterate peasant is no longer resigned to his fate. News of the abundance that can be created with the tools of the twentieth century has swept villages which had not stirred since the Middle Ages. We in the West sent the message. It has now been heard and believed around the world.

This revolution, then, is ours. It has returned, as it were, to haunt us; to challenge us to acknowledge our part in it. To have, above all, the common sense to foster it rather than reject it; to turn it to democratic advantage rather than surrender it to the forces of tyranny.

Communism is working mightily to forge the mass poverty of the underdeveloped lands into mass political power. We need more than military muscle and democratic preachment to meet this offensive. The dispossessed of the world are already well-versed in the vocabulary of freedom. The whole point of their contemporary revolution is that they have read the advertisements; they now want to buy and possess. They want not only to pursue the good life—they want to embrace it.

We cannot, therefore, hope to win the struggle for the future of the uncommitted by a campaign of democratic public relations. We must demonstrate the effectiveness of the free society by practical, tangible economic action calculated to move the underdeveloped and disinherited toward the point of economic breakthrough and takeoff into self-sustaining growth. And we must have the wit to perform this great task in ways that advance both economic well-being and freedom.

Words alone are not enough. Yet there is no reason why, in the context of economic development programs commensurate with the great need of the underdeveloped regions, we need be tongue-tied in our advocacy of democratic institutions and values. We must, on the contrary, be vigorous and eloquent in our espousal of the proposition that all men need—and can have—both bread and freedom.

The Communists offer the promise of economic security at the price of political and spiritual enslavement. Even their economic claim must be fraudulent, for under a dictatorial government, the rights of workers and consumers are at the mercy of political dictates.

We, on the other hand, cannot expose this fraudulence by debate alone. We must demonstrate by tangible accomplishment and day-to-day realizations that it is possible, within the framework of a free society, to defend and enhance the dignity of the individual and to find new answers to basic human problems under the constantly changing circumstances of a society that is being rapidly transformed by technology and science.

The strong, of course, have a moral obligation to help the weak; especially, perhaps, when the victims are being ground down by forces largely beyond their present control, which is the case, for the most part, of the deprived masses in the economically underdeveloped countries. Yet there are other dimensions to this problem than the ethical; other pressures at work than the pangs of conscience.

The privileged minority of industrially advanced nations might be indefinitely blinded by the complacency which afflicts the comfortable, were it not for the increasing evidence of impatience among the less fortunate—and the obvious danger that desperate men and women are now being offered an alternative (however illusory) to the slow and uncertain workings of the Western conscience.

History has, in effect, put the workings of our conscience on a timetable. The spurious shortcut to economic development offered by communism may not be impressive to us; it can be tempting to those who believe that they have nothing to lose but their hunger. It will be all the more tempting if the West fails to rise to the occasion with a development program geared to the magnitude of the need.

44

As long as the poor were merely poor, poverty could be considered as an ethical challenge. Now that the poor are no longer resigned to their poverty, now that communism is aggressively pushing its nostrums among the poor nations as a shortcut to the economic well-being made possible by technology, mass poverty anywhere on the planet has become a political threat to democracy's survival.

It has been said that time is of the essence in the moral struggle. Time is henceforth of the essence in the political and economic struggle for the allegiance of the uncommitted peoples.

This year, 800 million poeple will have an annual income of less than $100. Another 250 million people will have annual incomes of less than $200. In our time, no nation can be an island of security in such a sea of want.

The true dimensions of such poverty may escape us; statistics are frequently less a door to understanding than a screen between us and the fact made human. A few years ago in India, I stared into the eyes of poverty, mingling with a few of the 70 million landless peasants there whose yearly earnings amount to less than $20. I can personally testify to the human presence of such poverty on this planet. It is out of such personal experience that I urge a quickening of American awareness and general support for a more adequate American policy.

We must not, above all, let any belief in the inevitability of progress prevent our perceiving that the gap between the haves and the have-nots is widening. Our own technological development is outpacing whatever economic progress is being made in many of the underdeveloped countries of the world. In 1949, per capita income in the United States was 26 times greater than that in India. In 1958, it was 32 times greater. This is an example.

President Kennedy has issued warnings to the wealthy minorities within Latin America, calling upon them to institute the reforms and undertake the actions required to bring economic and social justice to their countries. The same warning might have gone to America itself, urging us to move more vigorously toward elimination of the great economic disparities among nations. Our obligation so to move is commensurate with our wealth and with our place of leadership in the free world.

The free labor movements of the world, united in the International Confederation of Free Trade Unions, are striving to shore up the values of peace and freedom by attacking poverty and its attendant ills in the have-not countries. We in the American labor movement are active in this ICFTU campaign because we see such poverty as a threat to the peace and security of the United States.

Peace and freedom simply cannot be secure in this country or any country so long as two-thirds of humanity live—as they live today—at or below subsistence level.

We of labor understand, however, that our efforts through the ICFTU are dwarfed by the dimensions of this problem. Nothing less than a co-ordinated effort by the industrial nations of the free world can cope with it. And of all the nations, the United States has the greatest single obligation to mobilize its vast economic resources— freedom's most formidable material asset—for this struggle. If we in America can harness our tremendous economic potential to this task, we can meet our needs at home and carry out our responsibilities in the world.

We are talking now about waging the peace. To wage

it, we need the same will, the same dedication, the same determination to brush halfway measures aside that marked this country's efforts after Pearl Harbor.

To wage peace, we need a greater sense of national urgency, a deeper sense of national purpose, a clearer sense of national direction. We need a view of ourselves and of our free society that goes beyond the material acquisition and comfort of what Warren G. Harding once called normalcy. We need to search beyond the huckster view of the meanings of freedom, in which the pursuit and possession of gadgets swallows up the larger ends of life. We need to go beyond this preoccupation with material means because if we narrow our quarrel with the Soviets to a contest between materialisms, we doom ourselves to ultimate defeat, since an absolute materialism has a natural advantage over a materialism which, while excessive, is only relative.

What, then, must we do? As I see our dilemma, there are several things we must do. They all lie in the realm of policy. They all involve a recognition that we live, in fact, in an era of problems which can only be solved by policy, not by a utopian faith in the blind workings of the market. They involve, that is, a measure of democratic planning, a fruitful combination of public and private programs directed at certain target or priority areas.

The business of America, in other words, is much more than business. Free man is much more than economic man, although his freedom and his humanity are intimately dependent on sensible and compassionate economic behavior and arrangements.

It is in this realm of bending economic activity to the service of democratic values that we distinguish ourselves

47

from the Soviets. In making our great economic potential serve democracy and freedom at home and around the world, we assert this distinction in practical performance; we break up the alliance between Communist subversion and the discontent stemming from poverty and hunger; we create a new alliance founded on a common faith in man's ability to conquer those ancient enemies. We find what William James termed a moral equivalent to war.

It is not enough any longer, if it ever truly was enough, to give the world a remote and isolated example of affluence among nations. The very economic and technological revolutions we sponsored have created disparities, aspirations, and conflicts in the world that threaten our national survival, make world peace insecure, and require the remedies that can come only from our unreserved commitment to a long-term program of investment in world economic development and democratic resurgence.

The shot heard around the world was more than a rhetorical echo. We are still contending with its reverberations. The question that haunts every discussion of American policy is, in essence, whether the embattled farmers and merchants of our native revolution are a dead dream of a golden age or a living inspiration with contemporary relevance. Have the American patriots of the heroic age become the household gods of a timid and selfish conservatism; or is their spirit still awake in us and available as a source of strength for an America determined to go about democracy's unfinished business?

When the echoes of our own independence struggle come back to us in foreign accents from Africa and Asia, do we recognize them—and are we ready to reply with solidarity and practical support? Are we united enough among ourselves to build here at home the expanding economy that will support such a long-term program of assistance?

Mr. Khrushchev has asked himself questions such as these about American unity and commitment; and he has answered them to his own satisfaction.

Perhaps even more educational than the personal experience of poverty in India was my personal confrontation with Mr. Khrushchev in San Francisco where I met and argued with him for four hours in the course of his American tour.

Mr. Khrushchev is obviously what we in this country call a tough customer. It requires no acute analysis to be convinced that he is cocky, crude, and confident. Nor can there be any doubt that he has a hard and shrewd intelligence.

The Russian leader applied that hard intelligence to an examination of American power and purpose. He came up with a prediction that communism would bury us, a prediction based on his finding that what we call our freedom is a mere anarchy of competing pressure groups incapable of resolving their differences for the common good in the absence of the fears and pressures of war.

It is deceptively easy to contradict Mr. Khrushchev; to point out that he drew his conclusions more from Marxist theory than from the evidence. The difficulty is that our refutation of the Khrushchev line must do more than satisfy our own subjective view of ourselves. It must make sense to the uncommitted millions who do not necessarily see us as we see ourselves. And it must make sense to us, not merely flatter our complacency. It must be a refutation by performance. It must consist, as I have suggested, in a series of projects and priorities.

First among these, I would put the project of getting America—and Americans—back to work and of so managing our affairs that our people and resources are kept at work as long as and to the extent that their full employment is essential to the satisfaction of growing needs in this country and abroad.

This country has been plagued for the past eight years and continues to be plagued by intolerably high levels of unemployment. Because our economy during those eight years did not offer work for men and women who wanted to work and needed to work, the whole nation suffered the loss of twenty million man-years of potential production, both in goods and services.

That loss is irrecoverable. Human labor is perishable. It cannot be stored like grain or steel for later consumption. If not used, it is gone forever with the winds of foolish economic practice. And the wealth and well-being it could have created are lost with it.

Our eight-year squandering of twenty million man-years of labor cost us $400 billion in national product never produced: the equivalent of $9,000 in additional income for every family in the United States. We threw it away as surely as if we had burned it or cast it into the oceans.

We threw away the productive years of workers' lives that will never come again. We threw away the possibilities of faster economic growth and with them the larger revenues that could have built schools, hospitals, clinics; renewed the blighted areas of our cities; raised teachers' salaries; provided scholarships for the proper education

50

of tomorrow's citizens; trained displaced workers in new skills; contributed to the waging of the peace in the corners of other continents.

In the last half of 1960, the American steel industry operated at about 50 per cent of its productive capacity. During those six months, we lost more in steel production than the entire output of the steel industry of the Soviet Union.

This is no way to argue with Khrushchev. This is no way to use the tools of economic growth. When we squander our potential so irresponsibly, we are wasting what might well prove to be the margin of democratic survival in the contest with tyranny.

Consider the contrast between our industrial centers as they are today and as they were during World War II.

The workers of Detroit, arsenal of democracy, outstripped Hitler's production in the Ruhr. The workers of Pittsburgh, of Gary, of the aircraft centers worked around the clock, six or seven days a week. There was a labor shortage. Grandmothers and grandfathers manned the machines. Every applicant with a pulse beat was hired. War brought full employment.

Today the workers of Detroit, of Pittsburgh, of Gary, and of other centers are haunted by layoffs and displacement. And they are haunted by a question that goes to the heart of our economic performance as a democracy: Why? Why does it take the fears and hatreds of war to create jobs? Why can't a man find work in time of peace?

I have never heard a worker proclaim that he was entitled to economic security as a matter of right. Yet there should be no doubt about the fact that American workers believe that they have a right to earn their own security;

51

that they believe there must be job opportunities enough for full employment in peace as there were in war.

This claim of the worker has been misunderstood and avoided. It must be honored, and to be honored it must be understood as a claim that the whole society must satisfy. The individual worker must contend with complex economic and technological forces beyond his control. Only the whole society, through a repertory of public and private actions, can manage these forces for the satisfaction of our national needs and, through meeting them, for the creation of full employment opportunities.

We are committed to such public responsibility in the Employment Act of 1946, which pledges the federal government to pursue policies essential to maintain maximum levels of employment, production, and purchasing power. As a practical matter, however, the Act has not been implemented.

If the Act is not implemented, we shall be in increasing trouble as technology advances and the labor force grows. It is a quixotic delusion to suppose that the blind forces of the market alone can balance our national budget of needs and resources at full employment levels. Adam Smith is dead, automation is making inroads in sector after sector, and we must come up with 80,000 new jobs every week of the next ten years of our lives just to accommodate the 13½ million workers who will be entering the labor market and to take care of those who will be displaced by technological change. We shall need, in short, 41 million new jobs in the next decade, without taking into account the job needs of the 4½ million Americans currently unemployed.

A few comparisons may serve to sharpen our sense of the magnitude of the employment problem. General Motors, largest manufacturing corporation in the world, has 400,000 employees. To keep ourselves employed in the next ten years, we are going to have to create the job equivalent of GM's total personnel every five weeks. Every two and a half weeks, we are going to have to match, in new employment, the 200,000 jobs now offered by U.S. Steel. Every week, we are going to have to offer new employment for 80,000 workers, the number presently employed by DuPont, the world's largest chemical company.

Technology is not waiting for us to find the social intelligence to deal with its impact. Breakthrough follows breakthrough. One of the most far-reaching has come recently in computer technology. The computers in the Wayne State University Computing and Data Processing Center, which have an impulse cycle of 3/10ths of a millionth of a second, are about to become old-fashioned. New computers will soon be available with an impulse cycle of 3/10ths of a billionth of a second, a thousand times faster.

Developments in miniaturization are such that the new computers will no longer, like the old, take up an acre; they will fit in a desk drawer.

As the computers get smaller, the problems they create get larger. We are only at the beginning of this process. Automation and computer technology already have entered or may be expected to invade every field, including the service industries and the ranks of middle management. It had been assumed until recently, it seems, that automation was the industrial wage earner's bad dream; it is now becoming evident that the new technology may

53

well become everybody's nightmare before it becomes that ultimate blessing which it has always been in the National Association of Manufacturers brochures.[1]

Questions of how to deal with the mixed blessings of the new technology cannot be left to the "pure" or natural sciences. No physicist is going to solve the dilemma of the displaced worker, or put together the dynamics of economic growth, or provide the perfect balance of work and leisure, in a neat formula.

We must turn to the impure sciences and arts of human behavior and relationship; to the arena where technical progress must be transformed into human progress. Even here, life transcends the academic disciplines; wisdom, sanity, and responsibility do not flow automatically out of knowledge.

Seymour E. Harris, the economist, testified to the dilemma:

> I have been at conferences with Presidential candidates and high officials where at first the assignment to the economist was to restrict the discussion to the economic issues and to leave the other aspects to the non-economists. But eventually the crucial question was put: What shall I do? And that often means a consideration not only of economics, but value judgments, politics, administration, and so forth. Economics alone will not solve problems of policy. An economist who thinks it will overestimates the importance of his subject.[2]

We are back, then, to a question of values. The problem of how to manage, by which I mean share, the economic abundance that technical progress now makes possible is neither a technical nor an economic problem; it is our old question of value and purpose. And because we have evaded it, we are victims of economic absurdities of our own making.

Consider this absurdity as it manifests itself in the appliance industry. That industry, for the past few years, has been operating at less than 50 per cent of its productive capability. Does this mean that every household in America is well supplied with washing machines, refrigerators, deep freezers, electric ranges? Not at all.

The difficulty is simply that millions of families who need them or want them are not buying them because they do not have the purchasing power to convert their wants or desires into effective market demand.

The problem of the appliance industry, written large, becomes the essential dilemma of our whole economy. We are living by the economics of scarcity in an environment rapidly being transformed by technology and science into an environment of abundance.

To live by the rules of abundance, we need to be able to use what we are capable of producing, which means that there must be enough purchasing power among consumers to buy what consumers need or want. Such a balance of productive and consumer power must be dynamic; as our productive power grows with technological innovation, the income of consumers must grow if we want to keep ourselves at work and our productive resources employed.

Such a balance involves a proper sharing among workers, consumers, and stockholders. And it involves public policy, because only through public policy can the needs of the whole community be considered. People want schools and hospitals as well as refrigerators and automobiles. The so-called private sector of the economy, acting through market choices, is incapable of deciding how many schools, hospitals, or highways should be built; how much of the national income should go for the renewal of the disintegrating core of our cities; how much should go for military procurement and how much for scholarships, teacher salaries, the preservation and development of open space for national, state, and local recreational areas.

The people of the country, using the instrumentalities of government as well as the instrumentality of the market, must make these choices and establish these priorities. Public planning for public goals has become commonplace in other countries of the free world. The European Economic Community is a product of such planning. France has had a planning commission since 1946 which serves not as a large bureaucracy but as a forum where representatives of the public and private sectors of the economy voluntarily co-operate in the formulation of development goals by industry and region. Between 1949 and 1959, France through this procedure increased its production of goods and services at an average yearly rate of 4.5 per cent; the 1960–66 goal is an average annual growth rate of 5.5 per cent. Since 1953, the United States growth rate has been an average 2.4 per cent annually.[3]

We need not ape the policies of others to learn from their experience; essentially conservative governments throughout the Western world have been drawn to the planned management of their resources for the satisfaction of general needs, not through any theories inimical to freedom but out of a logic implicit in the economic and technological facts of life as we are living them today and must live them tomorrow.

Recession, unemployment, idle capacity have come to

be generally recognized as man-made ills which need not and, indeed, cannot be tolerated in an era when their remedies are available and when democracy is increasingly challenged to apply these remedies to meet domestic and world needs.

Franklin Roosevelt's depression-era dictum—that policy must be judged not by what it does to help the privileged few but by how well it helps the many with too little to get enough—now has a world relevance; democracy will stand or fall by its success in implementing it, by its effectiveness in meeting the needs of the whole community. The market can meet only part of those needs; public decisions and programs must supplement and stimulate market activity.

One of the prime democratic tools at our disposal in the private economic sector is that of collective bargaining. It can be used more effectively than it has been used in the past to find practical ways to realize and manage abundance in the general interest.

Collective bargaining today is far from the level of maturity it must attain to perform these economic and social functions. There are, in my view, four principles which should inform a mature collective bargaining relationship.

The first element of maturity would be a mutual recognition by the parties that free labor and free management have more in common than in conflict; that neither can exist without the other; that both must cooperate for the preservation of the free society which is the indispensable foundation of their own freedoms.

Secondly, union and management representatives must discharge their special responsibilities as spokesmen for the interests of workers and shareholders in a manner which takes account of their common responsibility to the whole of society. This common charge upon them is paramount. In truth, neither party can hope to prosper in the long pull unless they both discharge their common task to further the progress of the community, of which their own progress is a share.

Thirdly, in order to meet this common obligation, there must be a common disposition to reduce the element of economic power in collective bargaining and to give greater determining power to the controlling evidence of economic fact. To begin with, the relevant facts must be on the table, rather than hidden, as is too often the case, behind the curtain of managerial privilege or trade secrecy. One cannot logically disparage the play of power in collective bargaining while at the same time countenancing the withholding of the data essential to settlements that balance the equities of workers, stockholders, and consumers. When any of the elements essential to an economically sound agreement are kept in the dark, moreover, somebody's equity is impaired, the forces of economic imbalance are fed, and the ultimate consequences are the general damage of idle capacity, idle men, recession.

Those who deplore the confrontation of economic powers in collective bargaining must do more than wring their hands and write indignant letters to the editor when collective bargaining breaks down. They have the larger obligation to insist that the means be found to let the relevant economic facts—the only alternative to power or government regulation—prevail.

The fourth element in mature bargaining is a single

standard of economic and social justice, which must prevail in the society at large if it is to prevail at the bargaining table.

In a totalitarian society, industrial peace can be maintained by force, in the absence of justice. In a society of free men, industrial peace is a product of economic and social justice. It derives not from force but from consent, and consent is not encouraged when there are too great disparities in the economic treatment of persons and groups.

I recall that when the UAW first proposed to negotiate pensions for automobile workers who were making an average of $1.50 an hour, corporation executives whose combined income from salary and bonus came to $332 an hour for a 40-hour week told us our members could take care of their retirement without pensions if they had the prudence to save for a rainy day. This counsel was given us with the confidence of men whose own retirement years were already secure, thanks to assured pensions of $25,000 per annum.

One could multiply instances of the double standard. As long as such a standard prevails, sweetness, light, and economic reason will not dominate collective bargaining.

I come now to two other basic priorities, which have to do with the depth of our commitment to democratic values; two areas where forthright action in support of our faith in man's essential equality and dignity will serve the mutually sustaining ends of keeping democracy alive in a mass society and enabling that society to realize its full economic potential. These two critical sectors are education and civil rights.

Our vast educational deficit has been called a scandal

and a national tragedy. We cannot assume the burdens or realize the human possibilities inherent in democratic life in a technological society if we continue much longer to tolerate the inadequacies and inequalities of educational opportunity that now mark our system of preparing the young.

Municipal bond issues for new sewerage have fared better in this country than proposals to increase our investment in classrooms, teachers, textbooks, and learning. We believe in sanitation and good plumbing more firmly than we believe in enabling our own children to cope with the hazards of life in the atomic age. If we persist in this folly, democracy will need no Russian gravediggers. We will, obligingly, bury ourselves.

The Soviet sputniks and cosmonauts did not spring full-blown out of the Communist Manifesto. They were the end product of a formidable educational effort of great depth and persistence. We should not let our opposition to Communist doctrine blind us to the great relative accomplishments of Soviet technology and of the Russian educational system that gave communism this great technical apparatus.

The Big Red Schoolhouse is geared to greater accomplishment in the next decades. Unless we move more purposefully in the United States, the Russians will be turning out something like three times as many engineers and scientists in the next few years as will American schools.

One danger would be to ignore this Soviet thrust. Another danger, equally great, would be to institute crash programs designed to emulate it. We need the engineers and scientists and we must see to it that our educational system provides them. Our goal, however, is not to develop a soulless technocracy. Our aim is more vast than the creation of a technically proficient society; it is to nourish the beliefs, values, and practices of a free society. If we emphasize progress in the physical sciences and technology to the detriment of those values and habits that distinguish freedom from totalitarianism, we shall merely be caught in our own better mousetrap.

When we judge our present educational efforts in the light of this double imperative to grow both in technical proficiency and democratic achievement, our failure is both staggering and frightening. Our inadequate educational effort has not enabled us to run fast enough even to stand still in relation to mounting school population and deteriorating facilities, let alone give us a national educational output commensurate with the mounting complexities and hazards of contemporary life.

Every newspaper reader or television viewer has glimpsed the desperate controversies and strategies of municipal and state governments as they strive to stretch inadequate revenues to meet growing obligations. It is difficult to understand how this continuing struggle to make ends meet maintains the vitality of local government or protects any essential rights of our citizens. What it surely does, rather, is deprive our children of the education which is their due, perpetuating the educational disparities among localities and states, and penalizing the whole nation to the extent that local or regional shortcomings are inevitably reflected as national losses.

This phenomenon was dramatically illustrated in the geographical distribution of rejections for functional illiteracy in the World War II draft. Those who failed to meet the educational standards of Selective Service were in most cases products of the states and regions with the most meager educational budgets.

We shall prolong this inequality and general inadequacy of American education into the next fateful years at our peril. The time has come to end the sterile debate over federal aid to education. The federal government has contributed to education since the founding of the republic; in some instances, as in the case of the Morrill Act of 1862, federal action has been crucial and far-reaching. Only the federal taxing power can insure equality of educational opportunity in a nation of fifty states with unequal resources.

The time has come to acknowledge this historic federal role and to give the states the federal help they need. Those who proclaim that federal aid means federal control would seem to have little faith in the vitality of our local institutions and our individual character. Nothing could be more damaging to both, in any case, than indefinite persistence of the present educational regime of inequality, of too little and too late.

In the matter of civil rights, our most obvious imperative is moral; yet here again our lagging performance has vast economic and political implications.

One hundred years after the Emancipation Proclamation, and despite much progress, there remains a considerable gulf between democratic promises and practices in our treatment of the Negro and other minorities in the American community.

Whatever the impact of civil rights in the economic and political realms, any discussion of it must begin with and return to our moral failure to mean what we say, to practice what we preach. We must, first of all, acknowledge that our moral obligation in this regard would be equally great even were we not engaged in a world struggle for survival; even if we were alone in the world with our consciences.

We are not, however, alone. And our moral lapse in the matter of civil rights, as most Americans have come to know, has left us exposed and defenseless to the charge of hypocrisy in the court of world opinion.

It is useless to claim, as some may be tempted to claim, that no people enter that court with clean hands. We have eloquently asserted our democratic credo before all men. We have set it unconditionally as our standard. We cannot explain Little Rock and the other outbreaks of racial violence in recent years by general appeals to human fallibility. I have been challenged in the matter of Little Rock in India and in Africa and I know of no explanation that can be anything but a lame apology when judged, as Asians and Africans will not fail to judge it, by our own democratic professions.

Our failure to practice the brotherhood we preach costs us dearly throughout the world. It tarnishes our moral credentials as world democratic leaders. It breeds doubt among the millions who are coming to nationhood and who are only now laying the foundations of the social order in which their children will live. They have seen that the West has no monopoly of technological progress, what if they should come to believe that our professions of democracy are a sham, that our belief in brotherhood is a sometime thing, confined to ceremonial occasions and denied in our daily lives?

The H-bomb may deter aggression but it cannot win the allegiance of these emerging millions. Yet it is upon their allegiance that the world balance of forces may well turn.

As the economies in the underdeveloped countries expand, the American example must come more and more from what we do to improve the quality of our democratic society, not from our material affluence or our technical prowess; not from our wealth but what we do with our wealth. Our world leadership must increasingly be a moral leadership exemplified not so much in words as in actions.

That is the world context in which our civil rights challenge must be viewed. At home, it is easy to point to the economic damage done to our Negro citizens by discrimination and segregation. We have forced upon our Negro fellow Americans a second-class citizenship that shadows every aspect of their lives. The Negro is victimized as a worker and as a consumer. He is deprived of the training that would prepare him for skilled and professional employment. For him, the cycle of recovery and recession hardly exists; recession is his almost continuing fate. Unemployment among Negroes persists at a level roughly twice that among whites. And this economic loss imposed directly on the Negro contributes, in turn, to the general insufficiency of purchasing power that plagues our whole economy.

Yet here again, the moral damage is grave; the moral failure is at the source of the economic wrong. We can and must help to repair the moral damage by political means: the enactment and enforcement of a good law to secure constitutional rights is one of the best forms of education in good conduct. This form of education is an urgent requirement if all our citizens are to enjoy equality of civil rights before the law. Juridical equality is an indispensable foundation for the equality that goes beyond the courts into the daily life of the community, the school, the church, the work place, the neighborhood.

The fact remains, however, that a more intense cultivation of hearts and minds, a quickening of moral sensitivity and intellectual awareness, are essential if the free society founded on this continent is to flourish amid the unrelenting strains and hazards of this revolutionary era.

The revitalization of the free market of ideas should be high on democracy's agenda of unfinished business. I conclude with a reference to this priority because I suspect that it may be the most crucial of all. The current resurgence of "know-nothingism" in this country, added to the habit of conformity that has gripped us so firmly in the postwar years, aggravates economic and cold war anxieties and may well paralyze our capacity to meet our new problems and opportunities with new thought and new initiatives.

We face many complex challenges unknown to earlier generations. Great as our founding generations were, they could not peer into the future that has become our demanding present. We live in a different world. The only predictable element in human life is the inevitability of change, and the tempo of change in our time has accelerated. We cannot reach out and grasp the future by staring backward, transfixed by the past. We need to see our own dangers and possibilities with unblinking clarity.

We need, for our unprecedented task, a coolness and courage and a readiness to consider the merits of conflicting proposals regardless of their source. These virtues can never come from the obscurantism and paranoia of those who inevitably charge conspiracy and treason whenever idea clashes with idea.

For the second time in a decade, the United States is being terrorized by a know-nothing crusade. An effort is now being made to conscript us into the fantasy world of the Birchites, before we have fully recovered from the moral and psychological damage incurred in our earlier bout with the irrationalism of the McCarthy period.

The Birchite complex is fairly easy to explain but not so easy to cure. It is clear that we are being treated to the savage attacks on former President Dwight Eisenhower and Chief Justice Earl Warren for their alleged complicity in the Communist conspiracy because the men and women who do Welch's bidding are like Welch in that they see conspiracy everywhere. And they build this sense of oppression and aggression to such grotesque proportions out of deep, unacknowledged fear of the complexities and difficult choices facing free men.

Driven by this fear, the Birchites have retreated into a fantasy of American innocence in an evil world. And this fantasy has been so colored by their social prejudices and economic conservatism that they situate their unreal, innocent America in an irretrievable past.

Their essential demand is that we repeal the twentieth century and go back to live with them in their golden age before the income tax and labor unions and such massive problems as the challenge of totalitarianism and rising expectations in the underdeveloped world.

I am sure there is a large majority in the country who reject this simple (and simply impossible) answer to complex problems. We cannot deter the Communist thrust as we would once have put down trouble south of the border, by sending United States Marines. We cannot repeal the twentieth century; we are fated to live in it. Our only option is to live in it intelligently or foolishly, with courage or in panic.

If we choose courage and intelligence, as I am sure we do, then we must shake off not only the fears and confusions of the Birchites and their kin but the timidities and conformities as well, which have more generally characterized American life in the postwar period.

We must not shrink from contending ideas; we must welcome the combat. We must not fear the diversity of democratic society or the challenge to create a unity out of its diverse materials. We must not shrink back into the past; we must move out toward the future. We must not continue to rely upon the negative pressures and incentives of cold war to sustain us. We must call forth the positive energies and visions of free men and devote them to the creative tasks of peace.

The ultimate deterrence to communism is not the bomb but the yet-unexplored dynamism of democracy. I have spoken of a few areas where this democratic dynamism must find expression; there are others. We must confront, for example, the great task of renewing our cities, of conserving open space for civilized leisure. We must create an environment of greater dignity and security for our older citizens. We must rescue our young people from the no-man's-land where so many of them lose hope and promise, between the years of childhood and adulthood.

To do these things, so worthy of doing, we must be more adult ourselves. Adult, not juvenile, delinquency is our greatest scourge. We ourselves must become more worthy of the natural blessings and heritage of this great land.

Mere affirmation is sterile. Democracy lives and grows by bridging the gulfs between its ideals and its practices. This is true now, as always. We have become too much the prisoners of the negative thinking of cold war. We must look more to our own work, our own possibilities, and less to what the Communists may do or threaten to do. Let us, as the wise Voltaire urged, cultivate our own gardens. They are wider and richer than we have lately thought. The images of peace, freedom, social justice, and human brotherhood are now available and tempting to all mankind. It is within our deepest capability, as it is our urgent need, to give these images the flesh and substance of fulfilment.

III

Decision Making as an
Economic Resource

by
HERBERT A. SIMON

HERBERT A. SIMON, Ph.D., is a leading authority
on the art and science of administering human organizations. He was born in Milwaukee. He has served on the
faculties of the University of California at Berkeley, the
Illinois Institute of Technology, and, since 1949, the Car-
negie Institute of Technology. He is the author of scores
of publications in his field, a consultant to various public
and private organizations, and a talented public speaker.
His books include *Administrative Behavior, Public Administration, Models of Man,* and *Organizations.* At the
time these lectures were given, he was chairman of the
board of directors of the Social Science Research Council.

Decision Making as an Economic Resource

THE BULK OF THE PRODUCTIVE WEALTH of our economy is not embodied in factories and machines but is to be found in the knowledge and skills stored in men's minds. In a highly developed economy like ours, technological progress depends primarily on accumulation of this knowledge and skill, and only secondarily on the accumulation of physical wealth. I predict that the store of knowledge and skill in our economy is going to increase—both in quantity and quality—even more rapidly than it has in the recent past. I shall set forth presently the evidence on which that prediction is based.

Introductory Comments

Before I develop my central thesis, that our productive wealth is to be found in the skills stored in men's minds, I need to make some introductory reference to the social consequences of technological change and explain what I mean by "decision making."

In dealing with very familiar things, we take their main properties for granted—hardly troubling to mention them—and attend mostly to the qualifying details. Thus, when we think about technological change and automation, we are likely to slur over the central fact of our economy, that it is immensely productive precisely because of its advanced technology. We take that for granted, and hasten on to worry about the dangers of unemployment resulting from continuing technological progress, or the problems of a future society so affluent that it will be buried under the goods it produces.

Consequences of Technological Progress

In any discussion of economic progress let us not lose sight of the central fact. Let us be quite clear that whatever problems the human species faces—in this country, in the underdeveloped countries, in the relations among nations—a necessary condition for the solution of its problems is the achievement of the high productivity levels that advancing technology is making increasingly possible. I say a "necessary condition," for of course it is not sufficient. High productivity, by itself, solves no problems and may even create new ones. Without it, however, the future of humanity would look bleak indeed. The United States of our generation has proved to the world that extreme scarcity of basic goods and services need not be an irremediable fact of human existence. The importance of that demonstration cannot be overestimated.

In order to keep productivity at the center of our attention, I am going to ignore the very legitimate worries that are so often aroused by technological progress. Unemployment is a legitimate worry, not only for the man who faces it but for the whole society in which he lives. Excessive affluence is a worry that seems more remote to most of us, but that can be real enough to someone familiar with the history of the leisured classes in our own and earlier societies.

I am going to ignore these worries because they refer to solvable problems. Both history and economic theory argue unequivocally that technological change may produce transient but not permanent unemployment, and societies are increasingly able to remove the burdens of that unemployment from the individual. We need to accept a fuller responsibility for these burdens than we have in the past, but it does not appear unduly difficult to do so, whenever the conscience of society demands that it be done.[1] The problem of affluence is a subtler one, and I am afraid I can only oppose my optimism to the pessimism of those who see original sin at the root of human behavior. The evidence is not really very convincing that increased leisure in moderate doses will be used badly by those who fall heir to it.

Whatever may be the best solution to either of these problems, the slowing or cessation of technological progress is no solution at all. Quite apart from the fact that it isn't going to happen, the misery it would produce would be out of all proportion to the ills it was intended to remedy. Let us agree, then, that technological progress is the one form of progress that humanity can reliably produce, that it is vitally important to the future of humanity, and that if it sometimes has harmful side effects, these can be mitigated without surrendering its main benefits.

Decision Making, Problem Solving, Thinking

One more introductory comment is needed—an explanation of the term "decision making" in my title. I have used it as a shorthand phrase to denote the whole range of problem solving, thinking, and choosing activities that are involved in productive work. I shall regard all work as "decision making" except the actual, final application of physical energy. I shall include everything under the rubric that takes place in the central nervous system of the worker. My reason for lumping together in this way all the activities of workers' minds will become apparent as we proceed. I observe in passing that what contemporary research is teaching us about the human mind suggests that the processes involved in the "decision making" of the worker on the assembly line are not really very different from the decision-making processes of executives. All thinking appears to have some fundamental characteristics in common that justify treating it as a single economic resource.

Human Capital and Productivity

Traditionally, economists have classified the factors of production as land, labor, and capital. When we think of technology, it is the quantity and quality of the capital employed in production that comes first to mind. We classify primitive technologies as Stone Age, Bronze Age, and Iron Age, and take the steam engine and the blast furnace as our symbols for the Industrial Revolution.

In what does the transition from a pre-industrial to an industrial culture consist? Most obviously, it consists in the introduction of a multitude of new forms of capital equipment—machinery, tools, means of transportation. A major aspect of the change is replacing man (and his domestic animals) by inanimate nature as the main source of physical energy for productive processes. Man remains the controller and the director of that energy, although he no longer provides it with his own muscles.

Physical and Human Capital

But this description of the process conceals the intimacy of man's relation with his artifacts. When man domesticated the horse, he did more than give up the use of his legs for locomotion. He learned a whole host of new skills—skills of riding and controlling horses, and skills of caring for horses. Again, when he acquired the automobile, he did not simply give up tasks he had previously performed; he took on new tasks—quite taxing ones they sometimes are.

Entomologists can often distinguish different moths by differences in the cocoons they make for themselves. But of course the essential difference is in the moths, not in the cocoons. The cocoons are different *because* the moths are different—that is, have different programs for making their cocoons. In the same way, changes in the physical equipment for production are symptoms of the corresponding changes in man himself. They are symptoms, in particular, of two kinds of internal changes in skill: changes in the skills of making such artifacts, and changes in the skills of using them.

During the initial stages of industrialization, spectacular changes generally take place in the capital equipment used in production. The amount of physical capital per employed worker increases enormously. The visibility of this phenomenon often leads to the erroneous conclusion that the accumulation of physical capital is the cause, or at least the principal cause, of the increases in productivity that accompany the industrialization. This interpretation, however plausible, is wrong—as we shall see. The increases in productivity must be interpreted as resulting from changes in the technique of production, in which changes in amount of physical equipment are one aspect, but in which changes in the nature of that equipment and in the skills of the work force are equally necessary, and more fundamental to the process.

The evidence is quite clear. Although the first stages in industrialization are accompanied by rapid capital accumulation, continuing increases in productivity in countries that have already reached a relatively high level of industrialization—the United States, Canada, Australia, New Zealand, Great Britain and Western Europe—have not depended to any large extent on further net increases in capital plant. Let us consider the American data.[2] Real output per man-hour has approximately doubled since the beginning of World War I. Over this same period, capital per employed worker, measured in constant dollars, has remained almost constant, growing exceedingly slowly. Several careful econometric estimates have been made to determine what part of the overall doubling in productivity could be attributed to the small increase in physical capital that occurred, and what part to improvement in the techniques of production. These estimates agree in attributing no more than 10 per cent of the increase to the growth of capital and the remaining 90 per cent to the shift in the production function—that is, to improvement in the quality of capital and to increase in the skills of the labor force.

Let me dwell for a moment on these facts, for I think they contradict rather sharply the picture that most laymen—and even a great many economists—have as to the nature and conditions of economic progress. Contrary to much of the talk about mechanization and automation, the overall capital-labor mix in our economy today is about what it was a generation ago.

If we look at the data for individual industries, of course, we will see that there has been an increase in the capital-labor ratio in most of these over the same period.

I would have a hard time convincing an audience in Detroit that this was not so. But an increasing capital-labor ratio in *all* individual industries is not contradictory with a constant capital-labor ratio for the whole economy. These two facts can coexist provided that the industries that are capital-intensive (e.g., manufacturing) grow less rapidly than the industries that are labor intensive (e.g., services), so that the latter have an increasing weight in the average for the economy.[3] And this is what appears to have happened. In particular, service industries that at present use a relatively small amount of capital per worker have grown more rapidly than manufacturing industries that use a relatively large amount.

Moreover, attention to factory mechanization and automation should not lead us to conclude—for we would be wrong—that productivity has increased more rapidly in capital-intensive spheres than in those where capital-labor ratio is low. An example will make the point clear. The practice of medicine is a labor-intensive occupation. Perhaps the most expensive piece of equipment required by a physician is a means of transportation. But the introduction of the automobile and the telephone enormously increased the hourly output of physicians (even before they shifted the transportation costs to their patients by becoming increasingly reluctant to make house calls). The savings from this increased productivity have not yet been shifted in any great degree to consumers, but that is another story. My present point is that improvements in the quality of capital may have as large effects on productivity in labor-intensive industries as in capital-intensive ones.

We should not be too hasty in applying these facts on capital and productivity to the problems and policies of the underdeveloped countries. There are still large sections of the world, inhabited by the bulk of the world's population, where capital scarcity is a major obstacle to rapid economic progress. Even these countries, in their development plans, have perhaps been excessively pre-occupied with capital accumulation as a key strategic consideration. But that, too, is another story. I am primarily concerned here with the future of economies which, like our own, are already highly industrialized. In an industrialized economy, the quality of capital and the quality of the work force are the main determinants of productivity.

The Quality of the Work Force

We must be careful not to equate improvement in the quality of labor with formal education or training.[4] It is true that most industrialized societies have moved very far toward universal literacy, and have depended largely on the formal school system to bring this about. The schools have assumed some of the training burden, also, that was formerly the responsibility of apprenticeship systems, or even of the home (e.g., training in cooking). But the vast bulk of the skill acquisition we are considering takes place almost automatically through direct contact with the productive equipment itself.

The passenger automobile in the United States affords a striking example of how the ubiquitous presence in a society of a piece of complex equipment allows most adult members of that society to obtain the skills of operating the equipment with a minimum of formal training facilities. (With the rise of driver education, this is less true than it was in a previous generation when even most automobile mechanics, as well as drivers, learned by doing.) The capital investment in the physical device produced—almost by mere contact—is an enormous fund of skills of automobile driving, automobile repair, and even automobile design throughout the population exposed to the device.

The same phenomenon can be seen today as the electronic digital computer diffuses through our society. Hundreds of thousands of persons are acquiring new knowledge and skills relating to computers—skills of operating card punches and data processing equipment, skills of writing computer programs, skills of designing and producing computers. If we could measure it, the total economic value of these skills would probably be several times the total value of the computers themselves.

At least a rough measure can be obtained simply by capitalizing the stream of income attributable to labor and capital, respectively, at the same rate of interest. In our society as a whole, about two-thirds of the national product is paid out in the form of salaries and wages, most of the remaining one-third as payments for the use of physical capital. Since most of the effectiveness of the work force in production derives from the kinds of skills we have been discussing—the skills of using the available physical capital—we can say that, at least in rough terms, the total national wealth invested in those skills is two or three times the total national wealth in physical capital.

Now we have already noted that we can have a steady increase in the *productive capacity* of physical capital without any net increase in the *amount* of that capital— simply through the gradual replacement of worn-out

79

capital with more advanced forms. Similarly, to increase steadily the store of society's human skills does not necessarily mean that we must devote more resources in each generation to training and education. Men growing up in our society today often learn about computers, something their fathers never conceived of. But one reason they have time to learn about computers is because they do not have to learn about horses and plows. Skills matched to our present technology are substituted for skills matched to the technology of the past. And all of this comes about with relatively little forethought or planning—primarily through exposure to the technology itself. Machines become their own change agents, carrying with them the information needed for their use.

Human Skills as Programs

To talk about the mass of productive skills that are stored in the minds of members of the labor force of an industrialized society, it is useful to borrow the term *program* from digital computer technology. When a computer is delivered from the factory it is just a big electronic "black box" having the potentiality to perform all kinds of complex symbol-manipulating activities. To change this potentiality into an actuality the computer has to be programmed—provided with complex sequences of instructions that tell it how to perform a variety of tasks. In practice, a computer is often separately instructed for each task it is assigned, but increasingly there are stored permanently in memory (on a magnetic tape, for example) a whole set of relatively general-purpose programs that can be called upon, singly or in combination, as they are needed to solve particular problems. A computer *with* its stored programs is a black box that has acquired the skills necessary for solving a range of problems (inverting matrices, for example, solving regression equations, doing factor analysis, and what not).

We can also think of the whatever-it-is that is stored in the mind of a human being, which enables him to perform tasks or solve problems of certain kinds, as his program. Various parts of this program can be invoked, singly or in combination, to perform a variety of tasks. Two characteristics of human programs deserve special comment. First, *learning programs,* programs having the function and the capability of modifying the remaining programs in memory in an adaptive way, constitute a vitally important component of the set of programs stored in human memory. In fact, most human performance programs—i.e., those that are not learning programs —are acquired not by explicit "programming" the human mind, but through the mediation of the learning programs, which have the task of elaborating and modifying the performance programs.

Second, while most of the performance programs stored in digital computers are relatively specific, and efficacious over only a very narrow range of tasks, the human memory contains, in addition to programs embodying specific skills, some important programs of a rather general-purpose nature. These *general-purpose programs* provide, for example, certain problem-solving skills, such as means-ends analysis, that appear to be used in handling problems in almost every subject-matter domain.

In our society, then, the bulk of the productive wealth consists of programs, corresponding to skills, stored in human minds. Many of these programs are quite specific in application, and hence are intimately interwoven with the structure of the physical technology. Other programs provide rather general capacities for problem solving in domains that are new, and provide learning capacity. When new physical equipment is introduced into production, the learning programs, operating by exploration of the properties and behavior of the equipment, enable human beings to acquire rapidly the new performance programs that are needed to operate the equipment effectively, to maintain it, and even to develop it further. Technology, in these terms, is symbiosis of programs with artifacts.

Referring to human skills as programs is less metaphorical than it might at first appear to be. During the past five years, a number of programs have been written for digital computers that permit the computers to simulate, in considerable degree, the behavior of humans performing relatively complex tasks. Detailed comparisons of the behavior of the programmed computers with the behavior of human subjects show the similarities to be very strong, in several of these cases. Hence, we now have reason to believe that skills are in fact stored in the human mind in forms that parallel closely the corresponding computer programs.[5]

Some Rapid Productivity Increases

Before turning to the future of productivity in the United States, we may use the analysis we have developed to explain several historical examples of rapid productivity increase: the conversion of the United States to a wartime economy from 1939 to 1943, and the postwar recoveries of Germany and Japan. These examples cast additional light on the way in which human skills enter into the processes of production.

The ability of the United States to increase its production after 1939 was of course due in part to the fact that its resources were substantially under-utilized before that time. A considerable part of the labor force was still unemployed, and capital plant was being operated well below capacity levels. Moreover, the war brought many new workers into the labor force. But to attribute the whole increase to these factors would be wrong. The existing capital plant—except for some parts of heavy industry—had not been designed to produce the new military products required by the wartime economy—ships, planes, and tanks. New plant and equipment were required for these and not simply the utilization of existing plant. Similarly, the skills of the unemployed workers, or of the persons newly entered into the labor force, were not the skills needed for the new production.

The design and construction of new capital equipment (itself a task making heavy demands on skills), and the acquisition of production skills by the labor force were the principal processes required to convert to the wartime economy. We may conclude that the principal underutilized resources that made the conversion possible were the *learning programs* of the employed population. In most societies, human learning capacities are utilized heavily in the child's progress to adulthood, but very much under-utilized in adult life. Learning programs atrophy rather slowly, if at all. In other words, there exists in the adult population a huge reservoir of "standby" learning capacity that can be called upon, by proper organization, to meet rapid or cataclysmic changes in the environment. In spite of constant references to the speed of change in our modern society, it is doubtful that more than a small portion of this learning capacity is used at any given time. The conversion to wartime production at the beginning of World War II was one of the rare periods when a large part of the adult population was called on to acquire important new skills in a relatively short time, and when, as a consequence, this hidden resource became partly visible.

My second example is the postwar economic recovery of Japan and West Germany. Both recoveries took place at rates that are a little difficult to account for in view of the extensive destruction of physical capital that had taken place. Most analysts of the process have commented on the "vigor" and "energy" of the population. The theoretical framework we have developed enables us to describe a little more concretely the nature of this vigor and energy. As in the case of American rearmament, the situation was one in which great use could be made of the populations' learning capacities. But another factor was present also. Much of the recovery involved restoring activities that had been present in the pre-war economy. Here the skills already existed, in large part, for designing, building, and using the capital plant, and hence the physical reconstruction could be carried out with high efficiency by drawing upon these existing skills. Provided the human programs are preserved, the destruction of the physical plant of an industrial economy wipes out only a small fraction of its total capital resources. Its recovery can be expected to be much more rapid than where the human programs must be developed from whole cloth at the same time.

Productivity of the American Economy

We have seen that the increases in productivity of the American economy over the past fifty years can be viewed largely as improvements in the programs of production. Partly, these improvements were imbedded in physical equipment—in new and more efficient tools and machines to replace older and less efficient ones—but without a significant net increase in physical capital per worker. But the new production equipment had the dual role of tool and of teacher. At the same time it turned out new goods, it provided the technological environment in which the learning of new skills could take place.

There is every reason to suppose that this same process will continue to be the basis for productivity increases in our economy at rates at least as great as those experienced in the recent past. Indeed, within the last fifteen years, four developments have taken place that are likely to accelerate the process and to bring the programs of men into even closer relation with the machines they use in their work. All four developments make essential use of the modern electronic computer.[6] They are, first, the use of advanced mathematical and other analytical techniques to improve business decision-making processes; second, electronic data processing, the automation of clerical processes; third, the use of computers to investigate human thought processes, and ultimately, to discover ways to improve the human programs for problem solving, decision-making, and learning; and fourth, the development of so-called heuristic programming methods that extend the possibilities of automating decision making far beyond the boundaries of the quantitative and the routine. Let us examine these four developments in turn.

Operations Research

Formal analytic techniques, drawing upon advanced mathematical knowledge, first entered industry in the area of engineering design. They did not extend much beyond the boundaries of that area until after World War II. Then, under such labels as operations research and management science, the revolutionary idea was proposed that many management decision problems could profitably be captured in formal models and solved by the application of mathematical analysis in much the same way that engineering design problems were. Within a surprisingly few years, esoteric tools with such names as linear programming, queuing theory, statistical decision theory, and dynamic programming had been developed and applied to problems of inventory and production control, marketing strategy, equipment replacement policy, and other management decision areas, mostly in the middle-management range.

Many of the real-life problems proved, when captured in formal models, to be beyond the limits of hand calculation. The digital computer fortuitously appeared on the scene to take over the computational work. In many cases, too, finding general solutions for the formal models exhausted the resources of classical mathematics. In these cases the computer again came to the rescue. By means of simulation techniques and so-called Monte Carlo methods, the behavior of the model could be explored numerically over a range of assumed situations.

In terms of our earlier discussion of the bases of

productivity, we may say that operations research and management science added to the existing repertoire of programs for making middle-management decisions a whole new collection of such programs, drawing their effectiveness from the analytic power of mathematics and the computational power of modern computers. Because this revolution in technique did not require new physical equipment, except the computer, which was introduced to perform other functions as well, it was not nearly as visible nor as often commented upon as, for example, factory automation. The former may well turn out to have substantially the greater long-range impact of the two.

Electronic Data Processing

Electronic data processing is simply a form of automation applied to the office instead of the factory. Like some modern forms of factory automation, it excites particular interest because it transfers mental rather than physical functions from man to the machine. Thus the program for a computerized payroll preparation scheme is stored in the computer and not in the heads of bookkeepers and clerks. In the new symbiotic relation between man and machine, the man maintains the machine, supplies it with performance programs, and improves and modifies these programs as conditions and needs change. The programs themselves are executed by the machine without the intercession of the man. One might say that the man holds the learning programs, the machine the performance programs. With this division of labor, the capital-labor ratio can vary widely, depending on how great and frequent is the need for program change.

The Study of Human Thinking

Under the two preceding headings I have described two contrasting methods for improving production programs. The first improves the human programs by incorporating in them more powerful formal analytic tools. The second transfers some of the programs from the labor force to the physical equipment. Are there other ways of enhancing the efficiency of the thinking, deciding, and problem-solving programs that enter into the production process? In particular, are there ways that can be applied to areas of decision that do not lend themselves readily to quantification and mathematization?

New techniques for improving decision making in non-quantitative, non-formalized, ill-structured realms have indeed been emerging; and surprisingly enough, it is again the electronic computer that provides the basis for them. I say "surprisingly," because most people think of the computer as a device that is peculiarly and necessarily quantitative and numerical. Historically, computers were developed as devices for doing arithmetic operations very rapidly. But in order to do this, they had to be given the power of interpreting and executing whole sequences of instructions stored in their own memories. In this important respect they differ from desk calculators—the program of operations for the desk calculator is stored in the head of its operator, and executed by him; the program of the computer is stored in and executed by the computer itself.

But the program instructions in the computer do not stand for numbers, they stand for sentences in the imperative mode—the computer circuitry interprets them and acts on them as such. When the instruction says "Add a to b," the computer must take the numbers a and b, and do to them exactly what the human operator of the calculator would call "adding." Only sophistry would deny us the right to say that the computer is dealing with the *meaning* of the word "add," and with the symbol-manipulating process denoted by that word.

Thus, a modern digital computer is not an adding machine or a desk calculator. It is a quite general-purpose symbol-manipulating device that happens, historically, to have been pressed into the task of doing arithmetic. But we know now, as the result of research over the past decade, that its symbol-manipulating processes are sufficiently broad and powerful in scope to allow it to carry out the same kinds of manipulations that humans carry out when they think, solve problems, make decisions.[7]

Computers have been programmed to design motors, to write music, to play checkers and chess, to discover proofs for mathematical theorems, to form concepts, to solve the missionaries and cannibals puzzle, to learn, to recognize patterns, to select a portfolio of stocks for a trust fund, to balance an assembly line, and to execute a number of other complex problem-solving tasks. Moreover, a number of these programs have been demonstrated to parallel or simulate, in considerable detail, the processes that humans use to solve the same kinds of problems. We are beginning to have, for the first time, a detailed, testable, and partially tested theory of human thinking processes. We can now begin to say what it is that a man is doing when he is "exercising judgment," "abstracting," "using intuition," or "thinking creatively." Even "aha!" experiences have been simulated on computers and the mechanism underlying them explained.

When we understand human thinking processes we

take a long step toward being able to improve them. Of course, that is no new undertaking. Teaching and training are time-honored activities aimed at the improvement, specific and general, of the programs humans use in their thinking. But teaching and training are activities that have had to proceed in the face of rather complete ignorance of the processes they were aimed at improving. As we come to know what kind of a problem-solving program a good thinker must possess, we will find all sorts of new and powerful techniques for aiding people to attain such programs. The instructional process will give up the shotgun spray of its traditional techniques for much more carefully aimed procedures.

If the bulk of the productive capital in our economy lies in the minds of our work force, as I contend that it does, the new advances in our understanding of human thinking promise improvement of first magnitude in the quality of labor, and corresponding rapid gains in productivity. My guess would be—and it is only a guess—that the findings of fundamental research in this area will begin to make themselves felt in application within a decade or less.

Heuristic Programming

We come finally to a fourth major development. As we begin to understand the methods that human beings use to solve problems not quantitative or formalizable in nature, still another prospect opens for using this knowledge to increase productivity. We can enlist computers in the decision-making process, not just with the classical analytic methods or operations research, but by writing computer programs that simulate some of the non-quantitative, non-formal, heuristic procedures that human beings use to solve problems. Such programs are commonly called *heuristic programs,* because of the important use they make of rules of thumb, or heuristics, in order to solve problems by highly selective trial-and-error techniques, as people have been shown to do.[8]

To be sure, man did not learn to fly by a slavish imitation of birds. When art seeks to replace nature, it is sometimes best not to imitate her too closely. In spite of these cautions, the prospect of writing computer programs that simulate human heuristic problem-solving processes holds out great promise for extending the range of activities that can be automated. Nor is this entirely a prospect for the future. Computers have already been programmed to do engineering design work (that is, actual synthesis of motors, generators, and transformers; not simply analysis of their performance characteristics) that formerly was handled by professional engineers. Heuristic programs have been devised for investing trust funds and for balancing assembly lines, to mention two that appear to be sufficiently effective to be used in practice.

The Economics of Heuristic Programs

In estimating the role that heuristic programs for computers might play in production, and the extent to which such programs may prove more economical than human decision making, we have to pay attention to the way in which programs are acquired or learned. The human being acquires his programs partly (perhaps largely) in an environment where he can try things and get feedback about the results of his action—he learns by doing. Partly, he acquires programs by reading or listening to other human beings. Usually some combination of these is required for efficient program acquisition.

If a human being invents a new program or improves an existing one, the two learning processes already described are the only ones available for transferring the improvement to other human beings. To the extent that he can write out a description of the program in a book, the printing press provides a cheap means for duplication of the description. But another human being still has to transform that description into a program stored in his own mind before he can apply it—usually not a simple process, for we are talking of skill acquisition and not simply memorization of verbal material.

Heuristic programs are usually acquired by a computer as a result of the efforts of one or more human beings who write the programs. However, some small experience has now been gained in writing learning programs for computers—programs, that is, that permit the computer to develop and modify performance programs by experience in trying to perform a task. Although computer learning is still far from much practical application, we may expect that in the future this will become an important means for developing new programs.

Once a computer program has been developed— whether by a human programmer or through learning processes—the economics of transferring it to another computer is quite different from the economics of transferring a program from one human being to another. The computer program can simply be duplicated—on punched cards or on magnetic tape—with as many copies as desired. Just as a new and more efficient organism, produced initially by a random mutation, can be reproduced through the copying of the genetic material, so new and more efficient computer programs, however they originate, can be copied almost costlessly. We have here a process for the multiplication of knowledge that will in time prove as important as the invention of printing.

The Division of Labor Between Man and Machine

Since man invented and manufactured his first tools, the boundary line between the part of the productive process he carried out himself and the part he assigned to his tools has been steadily shifting. But in the past, the area we call thinking was largely debarred from the tools. The governor that regulated the speed of the steam engine and the thermostat that maintained the house temperature at a comfortable level were important exceptions, but it was most unclear how they could be generalized to broad ranges of the functions performed by mind.

Now we know, at least in broad outline, how the generalization can be made. The division of labor between man and his machines will be increasingly governed by criteria of economic efficiency rather than limitations of technical capability.

And what do these changes mean to the future of our society? I find that many people are troubled at the idea that we shall understand the processes of human thinking, that we shall be able to simulate these processes with computers, and that in simulating them, we shall also be able to automate them. Some people find these prospects so worrisome that they refuse to examine and assess the extent of the progress that has already been made, or the evidence that this progress is likely to continue at a very rapid pace.

I personally find it difficult to share these worries. First, the idea that extensive automation must be or will be a source of human misery is based on fallacious economic reasoning. There is no connection, as I have already indicated, between the level of technology in a society and the level of employment.

Second, however painful it may be for the human species to acquire a deeper understanding of itself and of its mental processes, I cannot believe that its present ignorance is a blessing. It is a commonplace to observe that our knowledge of physical nature has far outstripped our knowledge of society and human behavior. But to understand society and human behavior requires us to understand how the human mind works. Surely the dignity of man cannot depend upon an unawareness of his own impulses and his own modes of thought.

Conclusion

My central theme has been that the main productive resource in an economy are programs—skills, if you prefer—that in the past have been partly frozen into the design of machines, but largely stored in the minds of men. While industrialization of an economy requires the accumulation of a substantial amount of physical capital, machines and equipment are more the external evidences than the real core of a technology. Moreover, technologically advanced economies like our own have long passed the point where further increases in productivity depend primarily upon new increases in the already high capital-labor ratio. Technological progress depends now upon improvement in the quality of capital and of the work force.

The modern digital computer introduces a significant new factor into technological progress. The computer, appropriately programmed, can share with human beings many parts of the job of production that earlier machines could not. Moreover, it can be used as a powerful research tool to gain a deeper understanding of the structure and development of human thinking. Hence it has strategic importance in two directions. It makes fluid the line that defines the division of work between machines and human beings, and brings machines to the aid of man's muscle. It also creates new knowledge about human performance that will enable us to improve greatly the programs that human beings use in production. Over the next generation, the digital computer will play a central role in increasing the productivity of the most important resource our economy possesses—its power of thinking, solving problems, making decisions.

IV

Education: A Backward Industry?

by
THEODORE O. YNTEMA

THEODORE O. YNTEMA, Ph.D., vice president-
chairman of the finance committee of Ford Motor Company, was born in Holland, Michigan. He was educated at
Hope College, the University of Illinois, Harvard University, and the University of Chicago. His career has included extensive periods of service as a professor at the
University of Chicago, an economist in several agencies of
the federal government, research director of the Committee for Economic Development, and consulting economist
to various business enterprises. Mr. Yntema was vice-president, finance, of the Ford Motor Company from 1949 to
1961. He is a trustee or board member of several educational and scientific institutions and holds honorary degrees from Grinnell, Franklin and Marshall, and Hope.

Education: A Backward Industry?

LEST MY TITLE MISLEAD YOU, let me say at the outset that I view education as much more than an industry. The heart of a school or a university is in the classroom, in the community of scholars, not in the business office. The value produced by education consists in part of higher lifetime earnings, but in the main it consists of the way men and women live their lives. And no one has yet been able to put a price on a way of life.

Nevertheless, there are good reasons for subjecting education to economic analysis, even though the analysis be incomplete. For education is both enormously productive and enormously expensive. In these Franklin Lectures, *New Horizons for Economic Progress*, my subject qualifies as a prime matter for consideration. Education produces the most powerful agent of economic progress—resourceful people, aware of the accomplishments of the past, and equipped with the ability to build a better future.

In his recently published study of economic growth in the United States, Edward F. Denison estimates that increased education—mainly an increase in time spent in school—accounted for more than one-fifth of the rise in total national output between 1929 and 1957, and even more important, for two-fifths of the rise in output per worker.[1] The advance of knowledge about how to use our resources in production accounted for almost one-fifth of the increase in total product, and nearly two-fifths of the rise in output per worker.[2] Education, therefore, has been the dominant factor in economic growth and in our rapidly rising standard of living.

In addition to its economic contribution, education increases our psychic income; it enables us to enjoy more things more, to live more richly, more creatively, and in greater harmony with ourselves, our environment, and our fellow men.

Since education is one of the most fruitful sources of many-sided progress, it is tempting to conclude that we should be eager to devote whatever time and effort and money might be called for to improve the quality and increase the quantity of education. However, as I noted before, education is very costly. It consumes not only large sums of money, but also, and more fundamentally, the time and effort of many people. And it is getting more and more expensive.

Since 1900, capital invested in the physical property of schools and colleges has increased from less than a billion dollars to more than $50 billion.[3] The number of students enrolled in schools at all levels has increased from some seventeen million to fifty million; [4] the number of teachers from less than half a million to about two million.[5] Students, teachers, and other employees of educational institutions now account for 30 per cent of our entire population.[6]

The annual cost of operating educational institutions, including depreciation of their plant, now comes to about $25 billion—four times as much in deflated dollars as was spent only thirty years ago.[7] Over and above this amount, the economic cost of high school and college education

consists of the earnings that young people forego while
they are in school or college. If we add this factor, we
arrive at a total annual investment in education of about
$45 billion a year.[8]

These figures suggest that it will be difficult indeed to
improve education very substantially merely by devoting
more of our resources to it. Surely, we cannot expect to
have much more than 30 per cent of our population engaged in education. Nor will it be easy for our schools
and colleges and universities to claim productive or poten-
tially productive resources amounting to much more than
8 or 9 per cent of the total available for all purposes.

Therefore, it is pertinent to ask: Do we make the best
use of the time and effort that now go into education? Are
the objectives well defined? Is the substance of education,
as reflected in the curriculum, well conceived? Is the best
technology used in the educational process? Do we have
means of financing that will attract to education the
talents it needs? Is education a progressive or a backward
industry?

I do not propose to answer all these questions, but I
hope to stimulate some thought about them. In the field
of basic or general or liberal education, I strongly suspect
that we have not really thought through what we could
and should be trying to accomplish. This is a subject on
which I have written and spoken on numerous occasions.
My thesis is simply that there are certain basic skills and
abilities needed in all walks of life to do the world's work;
that it should be one of the major aims of general or
liberal education to develop these skills and abilities; that,
by and large, education is deficient in this respect.

I would define these basic skills and abilities as:

1. Mastery of the scientific method—the ability to perceive and to solve problems.
2. Dealing effectively with people—including communication with them.
3. Organization—the marshalling of scarce resources for given ends.

If you will show me a man who can see and solve problems, who can deal effectively with people, and who can organize the resources he commands, I will show you a man who can be a success in almost any field and who can, when the opportunity arises, enter a new field and acquit himself with distinction.

One step toward improving the efficiency of education is to take a fresh and uninhibited look at our objectives. I do not imply that a person with the basic skills and abilities can overnight become a great mathematician, or physicist, or lawyer, or musician, or writer, or dancer. There are some careers that require special talents, and often prolonged development of those talents. But even in these careers the basic skills and abilities are usually necessary or very helpful. What I am saying is that most careers require the same basic skills and abilities, and in many such careers these basic skills and abilities constitute a substantial part of the requisites for success.

Let me say a few words about each of them.

First, the ability to use the scientific method. The scientific method is the process of seeing and solving problems. It involves observation, the detection of similarities and dissimilarities in phenomena, the tentative specification of categories and relationships based on observation and deduction from prior discoveries, and the testing of such tentative hypotheses by experiment and experience.

Logic and mathematics and statistics, in various degrees and forms, are required in particular applications of the scientific method. The roles of mathematics and statistics in the physical, biological, and social sciences are established. It is not so generally realized, however, that mathematics has widespread application to the ordinary problems of life. I believe we would save much time in the long run if all college students were required to be able to read and use mathematics and to understand the basic ideas of statistics.

I realize that this will not be a popular recommendation. Nevertheless, mathematics can be of great value to every person. Of all the disciplines, mathematics is preeminently the one that instructs us in the use of abstract thought. Through mathematics, we learn to generalize, to focus on the essential and discard the irrelevant, to find the general proposition that enables us to solve a thousand related problems without wastefully retracing our steps each time.

Mathematics gives us more than a particular kind of mental discipline. Certain basic concepts in mathematics and logic are directly applicable to a wide variety of daily problems. These concepts include, among others, equalities, inequalities, rate of change, rate of relative change, acceleration in rate of change, and particularly the conditions for a maximum or a minimum. We are forever trying to maximize or minimize something that depends on other variables.

I am not a mathematician, having taken courses only through calculus, and then having added a bit here and there as I needed it. But I did have the good luck to use mathematics. In switching from physical chemistry to economics, I found I could pick up overnight the basic ideas of neo-classical economics because I could read simple differential equations and inequalities. Since then, I have found mathematics an enormously useful tool in all kinds of problems, ranging from the theory of international trade and corporate finance to duck hunting.

But I had to learn this by myself. None of my mathematics teachers told me about the pervasive character of maxima and minima or hinted that the derivative of natural logarithms opened up the measurement of relative change. I learned the techniques in school, but not how to use them or that they could be useful in life and work.

If mathematics is useful now, I believe it will be essential to educated men in the future. Already mathematical techniques and electronic data processing are being applied to such varied problems as medical diagnosis, deciding how many trunk lines a telephone exchange needs, scheduling production runs in factories, and predicting the market value of used commercial aircraft. The growing role of mathematics in business and the professions may well force liberal education to recognize mathematics as a language and as a tool of thought and to establish mathematics as a requirement for all students.

The most important part of the scientific method, however, is the part most neglected in formal education—namely, *seeing* problems. Observation of phenomena, the perception of possible uniformities or relationships, and the specification of hypotheses in form to be tested—

invention, if you will—are given lip service but often get scant attention.

The scientific method is not the prerogative of the physical, or the biological, or the social sciences. Science and the scientific method are not the same thing. A science is a body of systematic, ordered knowledge. The scientific method is the process of seeing and solving problems. Most students in the physical, biological, and social sciences do not master the scientific method—because most of them do not learn to see, or perceive, or invent.

In my college days I learned as much about perception working on the farm and going fishing as I did in the classroom. I was, therefore, intrigued by some comments by Aldous Huxley in a recent issue of *Daedalus*, the journal of the American Academy of Arts and Sciences.[9]

Huxley urges the schools to introduce courses in "elementary awareness." He points out that "all our mental processes depend upon perception. Inadequate perceiving results in poor thinking, inappropriate feeling, diminished interest in and enjoyment of life. Systematic training of perception should be an essential element in all education."[10]

Huxley does not recommend fishing as part of the study of perception, but he does favor rock-sitting and flower-watching, which are pretty much the same thing. I think he would probably share my distaste for Samuel Johnson's remark that fishing is an activity involving a piece of string with a fish on one end and a fool on the other.

He goes on to say that "wise passiveness, followed in due course by wise hard work, is the condition of creativity. We do not fabricate our best ideas; they 'occur to us,' they 'come into our heads.' Colloquial speech reminds us that unless we give our subliminal minds a chance, we shall get nowhere. And it is by allowing ourselves at frequent intervals to be wisely passive that we can most effectively help the subliminal mind to do its work. . . . Watching and receiving in a state of perfect ease . . . is an art which can be cultivated and should be taught on every educational level from the most elementary to the most advanced." [11]

Second on my list of universal skills is organization, a skill closely related to the scientific method. In every science we try to structure facts into knowledge, and in every aspect of life we try to utilize scarce resources to achieve some objective in the best possible way.

In the various sciences there are common concepts and methods of organizing and integrating facts into patterns of knowledge. Note how pervasive are the following: counting, measurement, classification, rank, functional relation, balance of forces at equilibrium, and, once again, rate of change, acceleration in rate of change and conditions for a maximum or minimum.

Organization, in the operational sense, is the marshalling of scarce resources for given ends. It makes use of the same concepts and processes as those used to structure facts into a science. The proliferation of facts would make education impossible were it not for order and organization. Life would be impossible if we did not practice organization, and it is inefficient if we do not practice it well. In the educational process we learn organization in bits and pieces—hardly ever realizing that this is the essence of science and of rational existence. Organization

106

doesn't fit into the conventional curriculum very well, so it does not usually qualify as a respectable subject for instruction. Sometime, perhaps, we shall discover that the conventional categories of knowledge and research are not the only appropriate categories for learning.

Third on my list of basic skills is the ability to deal with people and to co-operate and communicate with them. Understanding and working effectively with persons and with groups is one of those highly important matters to which the educational community will not quite condescend. I hope that this subject, so important in every aspect of life, will someday be recognized as an appropriate subject for general education and a prerequisite for advanced study.

In order to work with other people, it is, of course, necessary to communicate clearly and effectively with them, to read and write and speak simple English prose, and to listen to it with understanding. I have often wondered why it is so difficult for the schools to do well the one thing that they have been trying hardest to do since the very beginnings of formal education. Perhaps the answer is to be found not so much in the way English is taught in English classes as in the way language is used in all classes.

Throughout his education, the student is exposed to a constant barrage of words well calculated to make him want nothing more than some escape from words. He learns from textbooks that have little if any charm, little interest, and little value except as purveyors of information. His own writing is too often confined to routine and repetitious drill. And when he is not reading or writing uninspired prose, he is often listening to teachers who lack sufficient confidence in themselves and their pupils to allow students to learn on their own. In these circumstances, it is probably no wonder that young people fail to develop the love for language that alone can give them competence in its use.

My complaint here is not only that students are overexposed to language that is ordinary or worse, but also that they are probably overexposed to language. In the provocative article I mentioned a few moments ago, Huxley stresses the obvious fact that education is almost entirely concerned with training in verbal, symbolic skills; that it pays hardly any attention to nonverbal skills and abilities that are equally necessary for a full life.[12]

In addition to courses in elementary awareness, other nonverbal skills that Huxley suggests as additions to the curriculum are "the indispensable art of letting off steam," and "the art of controlling physical pain."[13]

It seems to me that he is on good ground when he argues that we can and should be taught to use harmless physical safety valves to dissipate the negative emotions that lead to war and crime and family squabbles and "all the assorted beastliness of daily life,"[14] and perhaps also on good ground when he maintains that the mind can be trained to minimize physical pain.

But whether he is right or not, his recommendations suggest that football, woodworking, and sewing are not the only nonverbal skills that might have a place in the curriculum, and perhaps not the most appropriate ones.

However, I am not an expert on curriculum, and I can only hope that I may have stirred some disposition to question whether our schools are trying to teach what students need most, and what society most needs them to have.

Whatever we decide to teach, the next question is, how do we go about it? Do our present methods of teaching make the best use of the time and effort of students and teachers alike?

I have spent a good many years in the classroom, both as a student and as a teacher, and it seems to me that the biggest deficiency in methods of teaching is this: Instead of helping young people to find answers to their own questions and problems, we force-feed them what we think they ought to know. Instead of showing them how education can open the paths to accomplishment in the future, we ask them to memorize a representative sample of the lore of the past.

To illustrate my point, let me read from a proposal by Morris Kline, professor of mathematics at New York University. Today, he says,

Mathematics is presented as a finished product . . . What we should do is have the students learn to build the mathematics by starting with real problems— that is, they should find out for themselves, with the help of the teacher, what concepts either are available or must be manufactured to talk about the problem in hand, then formulate the mathematical problem which corresponds to the real problem . . . and then discover the process or theorem which will solve the real problem. That is, the mathematics should be built up in the very way it was originally built up by the mathematicians themselves. Teaching mathematics in this way would, I believe, orient and educate the students to tackling problems no matter in what field they might arise and in making effective use of mathematics in these problems.[15]

Whether this suggestion is feasible or not—and I think it is—it points up the importance of confronting students with problems instead of feeding them inert knowledge.

The problems used in teaching, I would add, must have a relevance to life that the student can recognize. The solution may reach as far out into abstract theory as the student and teacher together can go, but the problem must be significant and the results meaningful.

I do not say that teachers should limit themselves to answering questions that students are capable of formulating on their own initiative. This is the path toward narrow vocationalism and all the worst in progressive education. The task of education is not to answer questions. It is to help students to ask more difficult and more important questions, and to master ways of finding and applying answers.

The more that students can be brought to learning by solving problems that are real to them, the more meaningful to them will be the knowledge they acquire and, it seems to me, the more they can learn. All this seems quite obvious, and it is, of course, a commonplace that motivation is a central problem in learning.

We know this, and yet, is it not true that when we teach students economics, or mathematics, or literature, or physics, we teach them *our* subject, not an approach to their problems?—the problems they can experience? Is it not our unspoken position that students must supply their own motivation? We, the teachers, will patiently explain to them how important the subject is (to us), how fascinating its problems are (to us), and how much one has to learn to understand it. But most teachers, I believe it is fair to say, will not stoop to popularizing their subject by trying to make it intelligible in terms of their students' experience. The co-author of *The Lonely Crowd*, Nathan

Glazer, pointed out in a recent article in *Harper's* that the average professor of psychology "would think he was engaged in the worst kind of sellout if he paid attention to the psychological problems that concern the students rather than to those that concern psychologists." [16]

The result is that too many students learn to be clever at learning in the classroom. In a way artificial to their own lives, they absorb the subjects they are taught. And with equal or greater promptness, with or without benefit of comprehensive examinations, they forget their subjects again. The real pity is not that the facts fade away, nor even that the principles interpretive of facts grow fuzzy in retrospect.

The real pity is twofold: first, that students are taught so little of how to learn for themselves. They are brought into the presence of the educational apparatus, told that it is wise, shown how it doles out rewards and punishments, put to work on it, graduated or flunked, and sent out to live in a world that presents entirely different problems.

The pity, in the second place, is that our effort to make students learn what we have already learned is likely to destroy their own curiosity, enthusiasm, and imagination. In seeking to explain the failure of universities to produce a higher proportion of creative and productive scientists, the eminent psychiatrist, Lawrence S. Kubie, points out that "the small child has an extraordinarily free and creative imagination, which he manifests in his use of words, images, color, design, and tones, and in his general attitude to the world around him. Under the impact of many forces which operate in early life, this freely creative imagination usually disappears or at least goes underground."

"Later," says Kubie, "the inhibitory processes are further re-enforced by certain ingredients in our educational system, specifically by a fetishistic emphasis on drill and grill. In the educational processes of advanced scientific training, the destructive ingredients seem even more strongly entrenched. This would appear to be why so many gifted young students of science who have been carefully screened and selected undergo a profound attrition of their creative potentials."

"It has long been known," he continues, "that efficient learning is never hard, and that the degree of effort which seems to be required is never an index of the work which learning and creating involve, but is rather . . . analogous to the heat built up in a machine—a measure of the loss of efficiency." [17]

I must confess a good deal of sympathy with this viewpoint and with the student who resents fact piled upon fact, with little rhyme or reason, and assignments that take sixty hours a week, leaving no time for reflection, integration, or intellectual exploration of his own interests.

I believe, in short, that we can help students learn faster and more productively for their total life experience by enlisting their fullest efforts to learn for themselves. We need not fear that young people's lack of experience makes education in this way impossible. For, as students learn for themselves, their experience grows and their interest deepens and they are eager and able to take in more and more.

I think we know enough about good and bad teaching to bring about a very great improvement in the efficiency of our schools. But there is much more that we still do not know. We do not really know what intelligence is or what accounts for differences in it. We do not fully understand the relationship between intelligence and different kinds of creative ability. We know very little about why some students learn supremely well, while others of apparently equal ability flounder and fail. We try to keep everyone in school for at least twelve years, but we do not know how to teach the slower students much of anything. We know very little about the relationship between success in school and success in life.

I say all this, not to deride education for its ignorance, but rather to suggest that our schools have done remarkably well considering the necessarily haphazard nature of their work. I would like to suggest also that if and when we can find the answers to questions such as these, the efficiency of education could be increased far beyond anything we can now imagine.

Let me turn now from the art and science of teaching to the relatively mundane matter of educational management. Having some experience both as a teacher and as a businessman, it seems to me that many of the general principles of good management apply to both. It seems to me also that the business and financial management of education leaves something to be desired.

Indeed, if we gave as little attention to the technology of planning and producing automobiles as is given to the technology of education, I wonder whether our cars would run!

Jerrold R. Zacharias, professor of physics at Massachusetts Institute of Technology, estimated recently that only about 2 per cent of total educational expenditures is used for books, films, laboratory equipment, and other means of communicating "substance that does not come directly through the teacher's larynx." Even this 2 per

113

cent, he adds, is spent mainly for old materials that are already inadequate.[18]

The principal tool of American education is the textbook, and textbooks are seldom written by those who are best qualified to write them. Some time ago, I asked a distinguished economist, who was criticizing the elementary texts in economics, why he didn't write one. The answer was: "It's too hard work, and I enjoy more what I am doing." He might have added that textbook writing is not likely to bring distinction and honor in his profession. In fact, a good deal of the writing, and especially the revision of texts, is directed and even done by employees of the businesses that publish them, often by young men of little experience and wisdom.

The system of incentives is biased strongly against improvements in education. In our colleges and universities, the big rewards in salary and status go to the man who is distinguished for his research publications. I believe we need incentives for research. But we need equal incentives for improvement of the content and method of instruction.

Elementary and high school teaching is so organized that it cannot possibly offer the incentives necessary to attract and hold really capable people as teachers. Dean Francis Keppel of the Graduate School of Education at Harvard says: "My staff and I go constantly to Amherst, Williams, Harvard. We talk to the boys and we say, 'This is a wonderful trade. You want to teach kids. We'll put you in a classroom at twenty-one or twenty-two, you'll always have the same number of kids, no change in your job, no change in influence, the salary goes up because you live longer.' They laugh at us, and they're right—it's a lousy recruiting position." [19]

I don't know what the answer to this problem is, but I do know that until an answer is found, the public schools will never attract many of the superior teachers they so urgently need.

Our school year is still geared to an agricultural economy in which children were needed to work on the farm during the summer. But now we are no longer a country of farmers. What would you think of an automobile industry that operated only eight or nine months of the year?

Because of the large number of low-enrollment courses and the concentration of classes in the morning, few colleges make efficient use of their capital investment. One survey of more than a hundred institutions found that their classrooms are used, on the average, only 20 hours a week, and that they are, on the average, only about half full when in use. Thus, on the basis of a 40-hour week, classroom facilities are used at only a little more than 25 per cent of capacity. [20] If we make further allowance for the long summer vacations in some institutions that were more appropriate when ours was still an agrarian society, we find that utilization is perhaps as low as 20 per cent of capacity. Of course, we cannot expect anything like 100 per cent utilization, but it seems to me that we might reasonably aim much higher than we now do.

To my mind, one of the least satisfactory aspects of educational management is the manner in which higher education is now financed. Practically all children attend primary and secondary schools, and the bulk of the funds can properly come from taxation. However, less than half of our young people go to college. Most of those who do go to college are better endowed mentally and materially than most of those who do not go. We now make a gift to college graduates of educational capital, amounting on the average to about $4,000, which represents the cost of their education in excess of tuition charges.[21] Consequently, we subsidize a group that is already privileged.

All of us would agree that the country would benefit if colleges and universities had larger incomes, so that they could pay higher salaries and attract better people. Teaching is certainly as important as business or research, and education should be able to compete effectively with business and research for talent.

To take care of the surge in demand for higher education in the next decade, expenditures by colleges and universities will probably have to be increased by two-thirds or more. And even more funds will be needed if salaries are increased enough to attract many more competent people into the teaching profession.[22]

Now, any business would rejoice in a rapidly expanding market. It would have no great difficulty in finding the money to enlarge plant and attract competent people. However, because of the way it has been financed traditionally, higher education is going to have a very hard time indeed to find the funds to meet the increased demand. This, of course, does not make any economic sense.

Colleges and universities are chronically short of money primarily because our present methods of financing them prevent the full monetary expression of the

116

demand for education. Essentially, we place an artificial ceiling on the price of this much-wanted good, and then—especially at the institutions of highest quality and reputation—we engage in an agonizing process of rationing the available places.

Nor is this all. The large portion of the cost that is not covered by the price of higher education must still be covered. It is covered in part by driving college teachers into outside research projects and consulting. Another part is paid, in effect, by the families of the teachers who stay in teaching although they could earn much more in some other activity. But most of it is paid by begging the difference from the public or the state legislature. How good would our automobiles be if we had to sell them at half price and then go out and beg the difference?

If, as has been suggested from time to time, tuition fees were raised to cover the costs of education in both public and private institutions, and if loans on easy terms —yes, on subsidized terms—were made available to anyone and everyone who wanted to go to college and could qualify, the problems of financing higher education would vanish.

There is no question that the financial benefits of a college education make it a good investment, with a return comparable to that on investment in business. Consequently, there is a sound economic foundation for both a demand for, and a supply of, such loans. A market dealing in them already exists, to some extent at least. There are banks willing to make such loans and one or two brokers in the business of directing those who desire to borrow for educational purposes to possible lenders. But

117

the market is not now extensive enough, and the demand for funds would be much bigger if full-cost tuition were charged.

An adequate private market for such loans might develop simply as the result of a much bigger demand. However, it might well be desirable to institute a program of government guarantees of education loans on the model of FHA. Such a program would serve to stimulate the flow of funds, to keep interest rates low, to facilitate repayment over long periods, and to protect the lending institution against bad debts. It seems to me that under such a plan, repayments might well be spread over ten or twenty years or longer, with provision for cancellation in whole or in part if income failed to reach a minimum level. The subsidy of such loans can easily be justified by the benefits of education to society, beyond its benefits to the individual.

I have heard the arguments against this suggestion, and they sound to me like the kind of objections that are raised against any departure from tradition. Certainly there are some minuses, but the advantages are tremendous. Colleges and universities could compete successfully for the best talent in the country. Our independent institutions of learning would flourish. The huge state tax bill would come down. Government control of higher education would not be increased. It is even possible that higher education would be more highly valued because it cost more. And college and university presidents, whose primary job now is begging, could give their full attention to administration, to planning and policy making, and to leadership in education that we so desperately need.

My basic point is that a system that makes the costs of

118

higher education explicit, and gives people their choice, is probably the only way we are ever going to get enough of the highly talented people we need in college teaching, and the only way we are going to get a variety of educational opportunities reflecting the variety of different abilities and desires for education.

By charging the full cost, I think we will generate strong pressures for more education of the highest quality, for a wider range of quality and price, and for more efficient use of resources in higher education. All of this would be to the good.

Private, state, and local support of higher education on the present plan is inadequate and is likely to become even more inadequate as the demand increases. The remaining alternative is large-scale federal aid. I do not think that this would be the best way to improve and enlarge the opportunities for higher education. Let us be clear that what we are talking about is the appropriate locus of decisions on how much to spend and how to spend it. Government does not have access to any financial resources not available to the population at large; it is simply a question of how the money is to be collected and how it is to be spent.

I know that my proposals involve difficulties. For example, there is the specter of the mortgaged bride. Other things being equal, I should think a prospective husband would be well advised to take a bride with a college education and a mortgage rather than one with neither. But, of course, other things are never equal in such matters.

Whether my specific proposals are feasible or not, I do know one thing. The market is a wonderfully effective mechanism for accomplishing socially desirable ends with minimum social control over individuals and institutions. A completely free and private market in higher education may not be feasible. Nevertheless, I am confident that we could achieve more efficient use of our educational investment, more investment in education, and therefore more rapid economic progress if our institutions of higher learning did not insulate themselves so much from the forces and benefits of the market.

My central concern in these remarks this evening is with enlargement and improvement of educational opportunities. I suggest not a narrow financial, but a broad economic approach to these problems. Let us seek to improve the efficiency with which we conduct educational enterprises—not simply to save money but to provide the best possible education at the lowest possible cost. My suggestions may or may not be the best way to do this, but I commend to you the urgency of the task and the importance of the goals.

V

The United States and the Common Market

by
LAWRENCE H. SELTZER

LAWRENCE H. SELTZER, Ph.D., holder of the Franklin Memorial Lectureship for 1961–62, has been associated with Wayne State University since 1921, though he has had leaves of absence at various times for research and government service. He obtained his doctorate in economics at the University of Michigan in 1925. His teaching posts have included visiting professorships there and at the University of California in Berkeley. He has been an economist or economic consultant with a variety of government and other agencies for many years, notably with the U.S. Treasury, the Federal Reserve Bank of New York, the United Nations, and the National Bureau of Economic Research. He is the author of a number of books, including *A Financial History of the American Automobile Industry, The Nature and Tax Treatment of Capital Gains and Losses,* and, with W. L. Crum and V. F. Fennelly, *Fiscal Planning for Total War,* as well as of numerous articles on economic subjects.

The United States and the Common Market

THE CREATION of the European Economic Community, popularly known as the EEC or the Common Market, is, without doubt, one of the major political and economic developments of our times. Yet, in conversations with many usually well-informed persons, I have found certain misconceptions about it. For this reason, and in response to a number of specific requests, I decided that I might usefully devote my lecture to it. I have also decided that, at the risk of repeating some things that are familiar to you, it would be safest to proceed on the assumption that your minds are blank on this subject.

I shall start by indicating in a general way what the Common Market is. Then, to give greater depth to this definition, I shall sketch briefly its origins, character, and its progress to date. Finally, I shall discuss its political and economic significance for the United States, including its relation to this country's tariff program.

General Character of the EEC

The Common Market is the popular name for the European Economic Community or EEC. Created by the Treaty of Rome in 1957, it is, in limited respects, an economic and political federation of six countries. The six countries, distinguished by their common shading in the accompanying map of Europe, are: Belgium, France, Italy,

E.E.C.

E.F.T.A.

Finland

Norway

Sweden

North
Ireland

Scotland

Denmark

Ire-
land

England

Netherland

East
Germany

Belgium

West
Germany

Luxembourg

Switzer-
land

Austria

France

Italy

Portugal

Spain

Luxembourg, the Netherlands, and Western Germany.

The EEC already acts as a single nation in negotiating trade and tariff agreements with outside countries. And the members have committed themselves, among other things, to abolish restrictions on the movement of services, labor, capital, and business enterprises within the Community, and to co-ordinate their monetary and fiscal policies in order to promote high employment, price stability, and a balance of international payments in each member country. To carry out these and other provisions of the treaty, the Community is provided with legislative, executive, and judicial arms that are capable of being used in the future to achieve an increasing degree of political integration among its members.

The combined population of the EEC countries is only about 5 per cent less than that of the United States.[1] Their combined output of goods and services is second only to ours, if output is measured in terms of U.S. prices and weighted on the U.S. pattern.[2] Together they are the world's largest exporters. They are also the world's largest importers of agricultural products, and the total of their industrial and agricultural imports, excluding imports from one another, is greater than that of the United States.[3] Their natural resources are less rich than ours. Their greatest strength lies in the education, industry, creativeness, discipline, and skills of their population. In brief, the European Economic Community or Common Market is already a major new economic power in the world and, if it survives the inevitable early conflicts of interest among its members, it is likely also to become a major political power.

Origins and Development

I now turn to its origins and development. During and after World War II, three powerful forces came into operation to spur the Western European countries to seek a closer union than that which could be supplied by the traditional methods of consultation of independent sovereign states. These forces were:

1. A profound desire to make future wars between them impossible—particularly, war between France and Germany;
2. A desire to restore the political power and position of Western Europe in international affairs; and
3. A desire to enjoy the economic advantages that could be provided by continent-wide markets, such as were already enjoyed by the United States and Soviet Russia.

Let us examine each of these forces in turn.

At the close of World War II large parts of many great cities in Europe lay in ruins. The economic life of the continent was disorganized. The bare essentials of food, clothing, and shelter were everywhere in short supply. For the second time within a single generation, war had taken the lives of millions of Europe's youths and active adults—this time close to twenty million.

Throughout the Western European nations there was a deep feeling that wars between their countries were really civil wars that should never be permitted to occur again. Even during the war itself, various leaders of the Allied countries, in exile in London, debated plans for a European union that would make future such wars impossible—particularly between France and Germany.

126

The second force—the desire to restore the political power and position of Europe in international affairs—came into being some time after the end of hostilities. The urgent tasks of physical reconstruction and of restoring the means of making a livelihood for their populations had at first monopolized the attention of the war-devastated nations. But as Russia continued to ignore her promises of free elections in the Eastern European countries that she controlled, and grew rapidly in military and industrial might, her expansionist international policies became more clearly menacing. Suddenly many Europeans recognized that the United States and Russia had now emerged as the two preeminent world powers, eclipsing all the old European states. And they came to fear that their individual countries faced something close to quasi-colonial status in international affairs: at worst, occupation by Soviet Russia; at best, dependence upon the continued strength and goodwill of the United States. If the European nations could talk with one voice, they could be a third major power; as separate states, they were now minor ones.

During the debate in the French Assembly in 1957 on whether France should ratify the Common Market Treaty, Maurice Faure, the French Secretary of State for European Affairs, declared: "We are still living in the fiction of the four great powers. In reality there are only two—America and Russia. Tomorrow there will be a third—China. It depends on you whether there will be a fourth—Europe."

A third spur to European integration was, as I noted, the alluring economic advantages of integration. Between the two World Wars, the European economy had been almost stagnant. Growth in population and per capita income had dropped well below the average of the preceding thirty years. Tariff walls around each member of the patchwork of European states limited the scale of output and sheltered various domestic monopolies from external competition. These separate economies were out of keeping with the new speeds of transportation and communication and the new techniques of production. An economic integration of Western Europe offered the prospect of large tariff-free markets, which would promote mass production, specialization, and the stimulus to innovation and growth of a wider competition. The economic attractions of greater European unity enlisted the support of many persons who were sceptical of the political objectives.

A first concrete step toward European integration was taken as early as 1944, when Belgium, Luxembourg, and the Netherlands signed a treaty to set up a customs union among themselves, known as Benelux, scheduled to come into operation in 1951.

In 1952, the three Benelux countries together with France, Italy, and West Germany established by treaty an entity called the European Coal and Steel Community. This treaty eliminated barriers to trade among the six countries in coal, iron ore, iron, and steel, and set up certain supranational institutions for governing trade in these industries, though not in other goods. The agreement, embodying the so-called Schuman Plan, was deliberately designed to serve as a model for a wider economic and political union of the six countries involved.[4]

The Coal and Steel Community was successful from the start, and negotiations for a wider union followed.

After some disappointments, notably the rejection by the French Parliament of the proposed European Defense Community, these negotiations resulted in the Common Market Treaty, or Treaty of Rome, which was signed and ratified in 1957 and went into effect on January 1, 1958, establishing the European Economic Community. At the same time a separate but parallel treaty established a third community of the same six nations—the European Atomic Energy Community (Euratom)—for nuclear research and development.

Under the Treaty of Rome, the six member states undertook to create an Economic Community during a transition period of twelve to fifteen years divided into three stages. For this purpose, they agreed among other things, gradually

1. to remove all tariffs, duties and other barriers to trade among themselves by stages;
2. to create a uniform external tariff between the Community and the rest of the world, and to act as a unit in negotiating with other countries on external commercial policy;
3. to abolish restrictions on the movement of labor, capital, and business enterprises within the Community;
4. to co-ordinate their monetary, fiscal, antimonopoly, and social security policies;
5. to create an Investment Bank for Europe and a Development Fund for Associated Overseas Territories, and to allow such territories, mainly former colonies of the Six, as well as other non-member countries, to link themselves to the Common Market.

To carry out its provisions, the treaty established an Executive Commission, a Council of Ministers, a Court, and a Parliament. It is significant that of these institutions, only the Council of Ministers represents the individual nations; the others are agencies of the Community as a whole and involve some surrender of national authority from the individual states. Thus the Court may not be overruled by any member state in interpreting and applying the provisions of the treaty.

The members of the nine-man *Commission,* which is the chief executive and administrative authority of the EEC, are appointed by common agreement among the governments of the six nations. They are obligated not to act in the national interests of any one state but in the interests of the European Economic Community as specified in the treaty. The *Parliament* is at present made up of 142 members elected from and by the parliaments of the member nations—thirty-six each from France, Germany, and Italy; fourteen each from Belgium and the Netherlands; and six from Luxembourg. The treaty provides that the *Parliament* may later be elected by popular vote without regard to national boundaries within the community. The formal powers of the *Parliament* are at present largely limited to debate and recommendations and to the power to force the resignation of the *Commission* by a two-thirds vote of censure.

The *Council of Ministers,* consisting of one representative of each of the six member countries, is the ultimate policy making authority of the Community. The treaty provides that in the first stage of tariff and quota changes, unanimous decision by the Council is required on most important issues, thereby giving each member country a veto power. On some matters, however, the Council may and does act by majority vote, and the range of such matters is expected to be extended materially after the end of the transition period—1970 at the latest.

Thus the Common Market Treaty goes considerably beyond the reduction or removal of tariff barriers. By providing for the free movement of persons, capital, and business enterprise across national boundaries anywhere in the Community, for the co-ordination of national economic policies, and for legislative, executive, and judicial arms of the Community as a whole, it has created the instruments for some form of closer political unification.

When the Common Market Treaty was taking form, there was considerable skepticism in some quarters that it could ever be actually implemented. Traditions built up by generations of intense national rivalries were believed to stand in the way. Also opposed, it was thought, were the many business interests that might be adversely affected. But the highly successful operation of the European Coal and Steel Community and of various postwar international agreements on trade and payments weakened the influence of the skeptics. So did the sustained strength of the astonishing industrial rebirth and growth that had begun with postwar reconstruction. With the formation of the Community, this strength continued and a dramatic increase in trade occurred among the EEC countries, their imports from one another rising by nearly 50 per cent between 1958 and 1960.[5]

The impressive economic advance of the EEC countries between 1953 and 1960 (whether or not causally related to the prospective and actual formation of the Community) is indicated by the fact that their aggregate gross national product (in constant prices) grew 45 per cent, while that of the other European countries, including the

United Kingdom, rose only 26 per cent and that of the United States only 19 per cent.[6] The Community's share of total world trade also rose impressively. From 16 per cent in 1950, it reached 26 per cent in 1960, while the shares of the rest of Europe and of the United States remained constant at about 17 per cent and 18 per cent respectively.[7]

Under the Treaty of Rome, as previously indicated, provision is made for the admission of other European countries to the European Economic Community provided they agree to assume the obligations of membership, and provision is also made for associate membership on special terms of less developed countries and overseas territories. But a number of countries, while acknowledging the need for greater European unity, were unwilling in the late 1950's to accept the political commitments of membership in the EEC. The most important of these countries was Great Britain. Although Winston Churchill had dramatically offered to unite Britain with France in the dark days of 1940, and although many expected the British to lead the movement for a united Europe, the British refused, after protracted negotiations in the late 1950's, to accept the political arrangements of the EEC. Great Britain's traditions were those of a great sea power with far-flung interests, the head of a mighty non-European empire, whose traditional foreign policy in Europe was to maintain the balance of power rather than to take a permanent position with any single group. The British preferred to expand co-operation among sovereign states; they did not wish to jeopardize their relations with the other members of the British Commonwealth, which membership in the EEC might require; arrangements which provided England with cheap food and with tariff preferences for her exports, and provided the other members of the Commonwealth with duty-free or preferential entrance into the British market.

Sweden and Switzerland refused to join the Common Market because of a long tradition of political neutrality, preserved through two world wars; Austria, because she held that the postwar treaty establishing her independence required her to be a neutral politically; Finland, because of her fear of Russian hostility; and Norway and Denmark because of their tradition of a common "Nordic" front with Sweden.

But as the successful operation of the European Economic Community unfolded, these and other countries became concerned over being excluded. They feared a loss in their political influence in Europe, and they feared a loss in the foreign demand for their exports when the common external tariff of the EEC became effective against them. While still unwilling to become full-fledged members of the Community, they proposed a bridge in the form of an eventual free trade area which would embrace the EEC and themselves, and which could be joined by other European countries that did not wish to become members of the EEC.

After months of negotiations, however, the EEC rejected this proposal. While many factors no doubt entered into the result, it seems clear that the EEC insisted, in the end, upon confining the full advantages of membership to countries willing to assume the political responsibilities of membership. And this is understandable if a major ultimate goal of the Community is some form of political unification. An important means of promoting cohesion in any group is to differentiate it from other groups. Many persons in the EEC believed that a moderate common external tariff against all outsiders would promote this differentiation and cohesion without seriously obstructing trade with non-member countries. On the other hand, they contended that identical trade treatment for members and non-members alike would dilute the advantages of membership and weaken the bonds among the members. But there were also those in the EEC who squarely aimed to erect high tariff walls around the Community, whatever the economic and political effects upon the rest of Europe and upon the Atlantic community as a whole, and their influence could create a serious problem in the future.

The European Free Trade Association

The final rejection by the EEC of the proposal for a free trade bridge, so-called, between the Community and other European countries occurred late in 1958. The more important non-member countries quickly formed a loose association called the European Free Trade Association, commonly shortened to EFTA. The countries that joined in this association, distinguished by a common cross-hatching on the accompanying map, were the United Kingdom, Sweden, Norway, Denmark, Portugal, Austria, and Switzerland. Their agreement, signed in Stockholm in November, 1959, called for gradual tariff reductions among themselves on non-agricultural products; by 1963 they had reduced such tariffs by 50 per cent and had agreed to eliminate them entirely by the end of 1966, though, unlike the EEC, they did not plan to have a common external tariff.

134

It is widely believed that a major purpose of EFTA was to secure a better bargaining position vis-à-vis the EEC respecting reciprocal tariff reductions. But EFTA constitutes a far less powerful and less balanced economic unit than the EEC. EFTA has a population of only 90 million, of which Great Britain accounts for 53 million, as against 172 million in the EEC. Moreover, the EFTA countries export and import far less among themselves than with the Common Market countries.[8]

The response of the EEC to the formation of EFTA was to accelerate its schedule for internal tariff reductions and for a uniform external tariff against outsiders. A further acceleration took place in January, 1962: (1) all quantitative restrictions or quotas against industrial products were abolished among member countries; (2) agreement was reached on the general outlines of a common agricultural policy, which had previously been—and continues to be—a formidable stumbling block; (3) decision was made to move into the second of the three stages of integration; (4) negotiating as a single unit, the EEC concluded an important reciprocal tariff-cutting agreement with the United States; (5) the internal tariffs of the members were cut another 10 per cent to a level 40 per cent below the original one. Two other 10 per cent cuts took place six and twelve months later.

Several members of the EFTA—particularly Great Britain—now had serious second thoughts about the EEC. For all her strong ties to the other members of the British Commonwealth, Great Britain faced the fact that her share of the total external trade of nearly all the major Commonwealth members had declined considerably during the 1950's despite tariff preferences, while the share of the EEC countries had increased. As an export market for British goods, the Commonwealth members had fallen behind other countries in which the United Kingdom had no tariff preferences.

Denmark and Norway also became uneasy. Denmark has large and growing agricultural exports to the Common Market countries, while her exports get little benefit from the tariff reductions of EFTA. Norway's exports to the other EFTA countries receive little benefit from that association because about 75 per cent of them are already duty-free or subject to very low tariffs.[9]

Finally, in 1962, Great Britain, Denmark, and Ireland made official applications to join the EEC. Thereupon a long and arduous series of negotiations was begun by Great Britain in an effort to obtain certain concessions, including a longer transition period for the readjustment of her special relationships with other members of the British Commonwealth. Meanwhile the applications of Denmark and Ireland were held in abeyance.

A point of special difficulty was the great difference between the British and the German and French methods of protecting their respective domestic agricultural interests. Britain maintained low food prices by importing cheap foodstuffs from the Commonwealth with little or no tariff duties, and by paying subsidies to her own farmers out of the British treasury. France and Germany protected their farmers by imposing substantial tariffs on imported foodstuffs—higher in Germany than in France—thereby causing food prices in these countries to be well above the level in Britain. Farming is a flourishing and major industry in France. In fact, on the European scale, France is an agricultural giant, and she insisted that the Common Market's agricultural policy follow the lines of the French system. She desires a uniform level of internal agricultural prices for the Community as a whole, maintained by imposing tariff duties on agricultural imports sufficient to raise their prices inside the Common Market to the levels agreed upon, with the tariff collections going into a common agricultural fund. Since agricultural costs are lower in France than in Germany and in other EEC countries, such a policy promises to enable France to expand materially its agricultural exports to other members of the EEC, notably Germany, at the expense of agricultural producers in the United States and other overseas countries, and to some extent at the expense of farmers in other Common Market countries. On the other hand, since Britain relies upon duty-free imports from the Commonwealth for much of her food, she could not abruptly adopt the proposed EEC system without dislocating and perhaps causing lasting damage to the export trade of the Commonwealth countries, as well as creating widespread resentment among British consumers against the increases in food prices. In January, 1962, France secured the consent *in principle* of the other Common Market countries for the agricultural pricing policy that she proposed, but no agreement was reached with respect to the specific price levels. The German leaders, with their high cost but politically powerful farming interests to protect, refused to accede to as sizable reductions, particularly for grains, as France desired.

Despite the great difficulties that the proposed system of agricultural prices and tariffs posed for the British, the prospects seemed bright in the spring of 1962 that Britain's admission to the Common Market would be accom-

137

plished by the end of the year or a little later. If she were admitted, and Denmark and Ireland also joined, the European Economic Community would become an entity with a population of 240 million. What would become of EFTA if this occurred was a question that remained unanswered, though the magnetic influence of the EEC would then be stronger than ever.

These prospects were suddenly shattered, at least temporarily, on January 14, 1963, when President de Gaulle of France announced at a press conference that he did not believe Great Britain was "ready" for EEC membership in view of her continued demands for special concessions, and that he did not believe she was sufficiently "European" in outlook—though he expressed the hope that she would one day be admitted.[10] Shortly afterward (on January 29), France's representative on the EEC's Council of Ministers formally vetoed Great Britain's application despite the reported eagerness of the other five members to admit her. Apparently in retaliation for the French action, the other members of the EEC postponed approval of a convention proposed by France under which the former African colonies of the Six—mostly of France—would be given financial aid for economic development as well as liberal trading privileges with the Community, and they also postponed a meeting planned to discuss a common policy regarding foreign investments.

The French veto came at a time when other sources of discord were also becoming evident within the Community. As the tempo of economic advance in the EEC slowed down somewhat after 1960, conflicts of national economic interest within the Community had appeared. For example, coal mining in Belgium and Germany was hurt by the Community's fuel policy of encouraging rising imports of oil in substitution for coal, and these countries resisted the intensification of such substitution which was desired by France and Italy. The progressive reduction of tariff barriers between EEC members also began to pinch in some quarters. While all the member states nominally applied all the tariff cuts adopted by the Community, some devised substitute trade barriers. Belgium, for example, imposed a license tax on distributors of cheese and powdered milk imported from other EEC countries. France suddenly halted imports of Italian refrigerators while seeking permission from the Commission to impose a temporary import tax on them. West Germany enacted a law raising its "equalization tax" on a wide list of manufactured goods imported from manufacturers who are taxed less heavily in their home countries than German enterprises in Germany. The Belgian Steel and Blast Furnace Federation complained that German steel mills had even previously enjoyed a small price advantage over imported Belgian steel, and that this advantage would be raised to 2.5 per cent by the tax increase.[11]

Political differences also became more conspicuous. France's solitary veto of Great Britain's application for membership was publicly recognized by the Community as creating a major political crisis,[12] and the dampening effects of the veto upon the progress of the EEC are still conspicuous at the time of this writing. The veto crystallized the deep differences in the vision of the EEC held by President de Gaulle and other political leaders in Western Europe. Many of the latter emphasized the ultimate goals of political unity and liberal economic and political cooperation with other members of the Atlantic community of nations. To de Gaulle, in contrast, the EEC appeared to be merely a useful compact among sovereign states and one that could be readily dissolved if agreement were not soon reached on the pattern of a common agricultural policy.[13] He disparaged the emphasis of various EEC leaders upon further reductions in external tariffs and freer trade between the Common Market and the outside world. Instead he indicated a desire for greater emphasis upon regional planning within the EEC and for a self-sufficient Western Europe, presumably led from Paris. He called for a restriction of foreign private investment, particularly American, within the EEC, though Germany, Belgium, and other members were eager for additional foreign capital.

It is easy to exaggerate the significance of such internal conflicts, however. They are common in all families. Rivalry between states and regions and between the national and state governments was conspicuous in the early years of our country's history and is by no means absent today. Likewise there were important differences in political aims among the American leaders in the early years of the Republic, such as those between Hamilton and Jefferson. Political leaders commonly pursue a variety of goals, short- and long-term, and are usually ready to make necessary compromises among them. If the EEC can prevent truly serious disputes from arising too early, the solid growth of unifying common institutions and the pull of collective strength and advantage should be capable of creating a union strong enough to absorb even severe strains.

Indeed, compromises on the issue of British membership in the Common Market began to take form as early as July, 1963, when France agreed to join the other mem-

140

bers of the EEC in an agreement for regular consultation
on trade policy between representatives of Great Britain
and the six Common Market countries through the agency
of the Western European Union, which had hitherto
served mainly to co-ordinate defense policies. Almost si-
multaneously, it may be noted, France secured the formal
consent of the other members of the Community to her
proposal for liberal trading privileges and financial aid to
the former African colonies of the Six.

Implications for the United States

I turn now to the implications of the Common Market
for the United States.

The United States has been a strong supporter of European integration from the beginning of the movement.
Immediately after the war, moved primarily by compassion, which has always been a powerful force in this country, we made large gifts and loans to various countries, including the EEC ones, to relieve distress. Soon after, our
government concluded that a much better form of help
would be to restore and strengthen the European economies. As Russian policy became more antagonistic to us,
national self-interest reinforced our humanitarian mo-
tives. We saw in a united and economically strong Europe
a valuable ally in the Cold War and a stimulant to the expansion of world trade. A strong economy in Europe
offered safeguards against the encroachments of communism there; and it offered the promise that Europe would
become our partner in the task of promoting economic
growth and democratic institutions in the underdeveloped
areas of the world. Through the Marshall Plan, launched

141

in 1948, we promoted European economic integration by tying a considerable part of our grants and loans to the economic requirements of Western Europe as a whole rather than to the separate needs of the individual countries.

During the last few years, however, an undercurrent of criticism of this policy has developed in some quarters in the United States. As the new up-to-date factories of West Germany, France, Belgium, Italy, and Japan began to send increasing quantities of manufactured goods to our own and other countries, and particularly since 1958, when we first began to lose large amounts of gold because of an unfavorable balance of international payments, some people have said, in effect: "What an awful mistake we made. We spent billions of dollars to build up our competitors. Now they can undersell us, and not only in foreign markets but here at home. The Common Market countries have become so efficient that they are taking jobs away from Americans. We should be raising, not lowering, tariffs in order to give jobs to our own unemployed."

Now most informed persons do not share these views. Our aid helped to restore the European economies immediately after the war, but their great progress since the early 1950's has proceeded primarily under their own steam. They are not only strong exporters but are also important importers of American goods. And raising tariff duties cannot solve our own unemployment problems. Even the United States Chamber of Commerce, which often favored higher tariffs in times past, voted in 1962 to support President Kennedy's request that he be given power to eliminate tariff duties completely, over a period of five years, on goods of which the United States and the

Common Market countries account for 80 per cent or more of world trade, and to negotiate tariff reductions of up to 50 per cent on other goods in bargaining with any country for reciprocal tariff cuts—a request that was en acted into law.

There are three broad considerations that need emphasis in connection with the tariff questions raised by the Common Market.

The first is that foreign trade fundamentally means economic *co-operation* with other countries; the incidental rivalry is only a means to the most efficient co-operation; it determines which goods each country shall export and which it shall import. Through foreign trade each country is enabled to specialize in producing the things that it makes best and to trade some of them for things it cannot make as well. The result is a larger real income than would otherwise be possible.

Apart from the temporary effects upon total employment that are sometimes produced by tariff changes, as by all manner of other changes that are constantly taking place, the amount of employment in this country will be substantially the same whether we have high or low tariffs, whether we use our labor in more efficient or less efficient industries, whether we import less or more goods from abroad. For if we import more goods, we shall have to export more to pay for them. The jobs that we lose through larger imports, we get back through larger exports. And since our export industries are those in which we are most efficient, and our import industries are those in which we are least efficient, our real incomes and those of other countries become larger if we increase the volume of our imports and exports.

Because time is required for the necessary readjustments, it is doubtless true that reductions in our tariff duties could add temporarily to the number of our unemployed. But it is easy to exaggerate this effect. In a careful study of this problem, Walter Salant and Beatrice Vaccara of the Brookings Institution concluded that, on the average, a diversified increase of one billion dollars of imports (in 1953 prices)—equal to about one-sixth of all dutiable imports in 1953 and one-eleventh in 1959—is capable of temporarily displacing 86,000 workers.[14] This number is less than one-twentieth of the smallest cyclical decrease in employment in any business recession since World War II. Likewise, the United States Department of Labor has estimated that the amount of temporary unemployment that might be created through President Kennedy's tariff reduction program probably would not exceed eighteen thousand jobs a year during the five year period—a number much smaller than the temporary unemployment created every week by ordinary shifts in demand, technological changes, firms going out of business, general or sectional business recessions, and a host of other forces. As a matter of fact, in any normal year, some ten million employees are laid off or become unemployed for various reasons.[15] It is true, nevertheless, that some particular industries, localities, and individuals may suffer severe and lasting injury from tariff reductions because they find it difficult to transfer their physical resources and skills to more efficient uses. Toledo, Ohio, for example, is an important glass-making city. If imports of some types of glass from Belgium should increase substantially, some of the Toledo companies and their em-

144

ployees would doubtless be adversely affected. Following President Kennedy's request, Congress has sought to equalize the impact of such losses in part by enacting tax adjustments and loans in favor of injured enterprises and by unemployment and retraining benefits for displaced workers.

An expansion of our own and other countries' international trade is capable of increasing our rate of economic growth. In fact, international trade has been regarded by some noted economists as among the principal causes of economic progress,[16] or as a veritable "engine of growth." [17] It was a large expansion of its international trade that enabled Great Britain, for example, by importing cheap foodstuffs in exchange for mass-produced textiles and other manufactures, to increase materially its real income per capita during the nineteenth century. At the same time, the "newer" countries with which this trade took place were themselves stimulated by the availability of large and growing markets for their products to increase their own productivity and hence their incomes, and in the course of time to borrow techniques from abroad for the domestic manufacture of various goods previously imported. Economic growth in the "newer" countries was further promoted by capital investment from the "older" ones, particularly in such basic forms as railroads and other public utilities, and in government loans whose proceeds were used to provide basic governmental and social services. And the availability of lucrative outlets for capital benefited in turn the lending countries. International trade promoted growth not only by permitting international specialization but by transmitting to each participating country the impetus from growth in incomes, markets, population, and technology in any one of them.[18]

But many persons, including some noted economists, have feared that as various countries increase their degree of industrialization international trade will shrink because each country will make for itself more of the things it formerly imported. Although this view has a surface plausibility, the actual experience of the world during the past century, and right up to the present time, has been to the contrary. Industrialization has promoted both output and trade, and the international trade of industrial countries with one another far exceeds their trade with the non-industrial countries.

The first extensive empirical study of this subject was made by Folke Hilgerdt and published by the League of Nations in 1945.[19] Reviewing the statistics of the period 1870 to 1938, he found that the development of local manufactures in underdeveloped countries, by raising their productivity, stimulated their output of primary products for export, and, in return for their expanded exports, they expanded rather than diminished their demand for imported manufactures.

Likewise, a much more elaborate statistical study by Alfred Maizels, covering the period 1899 to 1959, arrived at a similar conclusion for both industrialized and underdeveloped countries. Maizels found that the industrialization of any economy increases its real income *per capita* and causes a much greater increase in its demand for manufactured goods. Although a portion of this increased demand is met by a growth of local manufactures, the

146

rise in the total consumption of manufactured goods is greater, and results in a net increase in *per capita* imports of the latter. On the basis of his studies, Maizels predicted a rapid growth in international trade in manufactured goods between the already industrialized countries as well as between them and underdeveloped countries. His calculations indicated that imports of manufactured goods by industrialized countries are likely to be twice as large in 1975 as in 1959, and that they are likely to rise by 50 to 90 per cent for non-industrialized economies, and by 25 to 75 per cent for semi-industrialized ones. Such an expansion of international trade, with its beneficent effects upon real incomes and its stimulus to economic growth in all the participating countries, may well be regarded as one of the new horizons of economic progress.

A second broad consideration is that *now* is the best time to further the adoption of international policies that would facilitate such an expansion. Between its formation in 1959 and the middle of 1963, the Common Market countries progressed about three-fifths of the distance towards a common external tariff as well as three-fifths of the distance towards the complete elimination of tariff barriers among themselves—two and one-half years ahead of the original schedule in both respects. Nevertheless the EEC's external trade policies have yet to crystallize. In its last tariff agreement with the United States, concluded in 1962 under the General Agreement on Trade and Tariffs (GATT, of which nearly all important trading countries are members), the EEC displayed a promising willingness to reduce her industrial tariffs in return for reciprocal tariff cuts by us. President Kennedy has been given wide powers to cut tariffs by the Trade Expansion Act of 1962. Another round of tariff negotiations under GATT is scheduled for 1964.

This time the highly restrictive policies of the Common Market countries against imports of agricultural products will vie with industrial tariffs as subjects of contention and negotiation. The outcome of these negotiations may well color the EEC's external trade relations for some time to come. Although some Common Market countries could doubtless gain substantial economic benefits by increasing their agricultural imports and releasing thousands of farm workers to more productive employment, a contrary policy is encouraged by a long tradition of subsidizing the growing of food at home (originally for protection in the event of war), and by the political strength of local farming interests. Hence EEC concessions in this area are likely to be made grudgingly.

With respect to tariffs on other goods, however, a good omen was given by a decision of the Common Market's Council of Ministers not long before the EEC's scheduled common external tariff adjustments of July 1, 1963, to make these adjustments on the basis of the average original external tariff *reduced by 20 per cent.* In other words, the EEC gave what has been termed an "advance payment" on the 1964 tariff negotiations with the United States and others. This "advance payment" could, of course, be rescinded if satisfactory reciprocal concessions are not obtained.

We have an important stake in the forthcoming negotiations besides our general interest in the expansion of world trade. The Common Market countries now absorb about one-fourth of total United States commercial exports—about $2.5 billion of industrial goods and about $1.2 billion of agricultural products. Unless we can negotiate reciprocal tariff reductions with them, we face a loss of a portion of this major export market as the EEC progressively nears its goal of a common external tariff. On the other hand, more liberal access to this huge market, which, as I noted earlier, has a population nearly as large as our own, can be enormously stimulating to American industry—and not only by offering greater outlets for our products. The goods we import in return can also be highly stimulating to our technology besides adding to the variety of products available to American consumers and American business. A few years ago—in 1959—the United States had a year in which some 668,000 foreign-made automobiles, mostly "compacts," were imported into this country. Our own manufacturers promptly learned their lesson. They introduced their own small cars. So-called compact cars in recent years have accounted for approximately one-third of American automobile output, and annual imports of foreign cars, while down to little more than one-half of their 1959 volume, continue to add the spice of novelty and variety to our domestic market.

Both liberalizing and restrictive commercial policies on the part of nations tend to be contagious. The readier any one of them becomes to admit the goods of others, the readier others tend to become to lower their own trade barriers; and *vice versa.* This is not surprising, because in the long run every country must pay for its imports by exports. If other nations are increasing their restrictions against foreign goods, each country tends to become increasingly concerned about its ability to pay for its essential imports by its exports; hence it is tempted to restrict "unnecessary" or total imports by one means or another. But if other nations are reducing their barriers against foreign goods, each country can feel more confident about its ability to pay for essential imports by its exports, and hence can feel free to lower its own restrictions.

Since the end of World War II, liberalizing tendencies have been more widespread and more pronounced than at any previous time. These have been fostered by international agreements, such as GATT and the Organizations for Economic Co-operation and Development (OECD), and its predecessor, the Organization for European Economic Co-operation (OEEC). A key provision of GATT is the "most favored nation clause," which provides (with escape clauses, however) that every member of GATT is entitled to every tariff concession made by any of the parties to any other member. In this way the benefits of any reciprocal tariff reductions negotiated between any two countries or groups of countries are, subject to certain exceptions, automatically extended to all the other members of GATT, now membering thirty-five countries. Regional reductions in trade barriers are also being promoted by the movement towards regional customs unions, or internal free trade among members of a group of nations. The European Economic Community and the European Free Trade Association are the most prominent examples, but others are to be found in Central and South America and in Africa. Exemption from the "most favored nation" clause is granted to GATT members for the purpose of confining the complete elimination of tariff barriers to fellow members of a customs union.

My concluding consideration is the most important one. The European Economic Community is, in a sense, patterned on the United States. We have shown the way. The EEC is copying our country-wide free market, and some elements of our federated political structure. It has thus far displayed a surprizing liberality in reducing barriers to trade with us and other outside countries. The EEC nations broadly share our political ideals. United in the Common Market, they constitute a far more valuable political ally and trading partner than as separate nations.

What should be our relationship to the Common Market? Some people mistakenly think that we should become a member. This would not serve the EEC's purposes nor our own. The EEC exists to strengthen *Europe's* political and economic stature—to make Europe more nearly equal to the United States and Russia. We, on our part, have neither the desire nor the competence to participate in the resolution of the detailed internal problems of political and economic integration in Europe, nor do we wish to commit our own country to all the domestic policies that the European Economic Community may find appropriate for itself.

I think our relationship should be that of friendly cooperation and competition between different but allied political and economic units. Each should be free to develop in its own way, and to cherish its differences. But we should recognize that we are allied by broad common goals which we foster through our common membership in such international organizations as NATO, GATT, OTC, the UN and perhaps others to come.

I emphasize our common goals because the free societies of the West face threats enough even if they stand united in their broad political interests. There is the threat of nuclear weapons in unfriendly hands. There is the difficult task of dealing constructively with the revolution of rising expectations in the underdeveloped "have-not" nations of the world. There is the problem of dealing with fanatical dictatorships of left or right.

Our best chance of preserving and extending Western democratic ideals in the face of these challenges lies in economic as well as political co-operation with the great democracies of Western Europe. Through its unifying and strengthening influence upon much of Europe, the Common Market is capable of becoming a most effective partner of the United States in facilitating such co-operation.

References

INTRODUCTION

1. U.S. Department of Agriculture, Statistical Bulletin No. 233, *Changes in Farm Production and Efficiency* (July 1961), Table 21. I have abstracted from exports and imports of agricultural products, both of which increased substantially between 1910 and 1960, but by roughly similar amounts and proportions.

2. *Ibid.*

3. *Ibid.*

4. Estimate based on John W. Kendrick, *Productivity Trends in the United States*, National Bureau of Economic Research (Princeton University Press, 1961), Table D-7, p. 431, extrapolated to 1962 by Federal Reserve Board Index of Industrial Production. Kendrick's indexes were in turn built upon those constructed by Solomon Fabricant in his *The Output of Manufacturing Industries in the United States, 1899–1937* (Washington, D.C.: National Bureau of Economic Research 1940).

I. PROBLEMS OF THE AMERICAN ECONOMY—HARD AND EASY

1. Part of this section is adapted from P. A. Samuelson, "Economic Policy for 1962," *Review of Economics and Statistics*, Vol. XLIV (February 1962) , pp. 3–6.

2. Warning: If a statistician measured the behavior of money wages in comparison with the behavior of labor productivity during such a period, he would find that money wages were far outstripping real productivity. Yet we know that this is a classical case of demand-pull. This shows that there is a serious pitfall in the commonly-met-with argument that goes as follows. "Any increase in money wages faster than the increase in real physical productivity of labor must be an indication of wage-push inflation; and the proper therapy for it must be found in some kind of control over trade unions and the wage-bargaining process."

II. PRIORITIES FOR FREEDOM'S SURVIVAL

1. Donald M. Michael, "Cybernation: The Silent Conquest," a report to the Center for the Study of Democratic Institutions (Santa Barbara, California, 1962).
2. Seymour E. Harris, "President Kennedy's Economics," *New Republic*, October 30, 1961, p. 13.
3. After this lecture was given the *New York Times*, April 11, 1962, published the following passage in a story on an OECD analysis of the American economy:

United States economic growth was much slower than that in Western Europe in the last decade because of "inadequate pressure of demand," according to a unanimous report by analysts of the twenty-nation Organization for Economic Cooperation and Development.

"Rapid economic growth will not take place unless an adequate pressure of demand on productive resources is maintained," the report said, continuing:

"Maintenance of such a pressure is within the control of governments, at least in the larger countries."

The report was drafted by a group of representatives of all twenty members of O.E.C.D. assigned to find out why some of the Atlantic countries grew much faster than others in the Nineteen Fifties. The continental European countries, with few exceptions, grew rapidly, whereas the United States, Britain and Canada grew slowly.

III. DECISION MAKING AS AN ECONOMIC RESOURCE

1. I have discussed the relation of technological progress to employment at greater length in "The Corporation: Will It Be Managed by Machines?", Anshen and Bach (eds.), *Management and Corporations 1985* (McGraw-Hill, 1960).
2. For a fuller treatment of the matters discussed in this paragraph, see Robert M. Solow, "Technical Change and the Aggregate Production Function," *Review of Economics and Statistics*, 39: 312–320 (1957). The concept of "amount of capital" is a tricky one, but Edward F. Denison has shown how an appropriate definition and measurement procedure can be constructed, in "Theoretical Aspects of Quality Change, Capital Consumption, and Net Capital Formation" in *Problems of Capital Formation, Studies in Income and Wealth*, Vol. 19 (Princeton University Press, 1957), pp. 215–60.

3. Let R_M, R_S, and R_T be the capital-labor ratios in manufacturing, services, and the economy, respectively; and let L_M and L_S be the fractions of the labor force in manufacturing and services, respectively. Then, by definition, $R_T = R_M L_M + R_S L_S$. If $R_S < R_M$, and if L_S grows more rapidly than L_M, then R_T will decrease even if both R_M and R_S are growing slowly, for $dR_T = (R_M - R_S)dL + (L_M dR_M + L_S dR_S)$.

4. Economists have been paying increasing attention recently to the quality of labor as a factor in technological progress. However, most of the discussion has centered on formal education as a process for investing in skills. See, for example, T. W. Schultz's presidential address to the American Economic Association, "Investment in Human Capital," *American Economic Review*, 51 (March 1961), pp. 1–17.

The present paper takes the quite different point of view that most of the economically relevant learning takes place "on the job," in the interaction between the work force and the technology. It should further be emphasized here that by "work force" we mean the technical, professional, and administrative employees as well as the blue collar workers. What is learned by the work force is not merely how to operate the machines and perform particular production processes, but how to design and maintain the machines and how to organize productive work.

5. See Allen Newell and Herbert A. Simon, "Computer Simulation of Human Thinking," *Science*, 134 (December 22, 1962) pp. 2011–17.

6. More detail on the matters discussed in the following paragraphs will be found in Herbert A. Simon, *The New Science of Management Decision* (Harper and Brothers, 1960).

7. See references cited in the two previous footnotes.

8. See references cited in footnotes 5 and 6.

IV. EDUCATION: A BACKWARD INDUSTRY?

1. Edward F. Denison, *The Sources of Economic Growth in the United States*, Committee for Economic Development (New York City, 1962) pp. 267, 271 (and Tables 31, 33).

2. *Ibid.*, pp. 268, 272 (and Tables 31, 33).

3. Theodore W. Schultz, "Capital Formation by Education," *Journal of Political Economy*, Vol. LXVIII, No. 6 (December, 1960), Tables 3 and 4, pp. 578, 579. Estimates for 1958 and 1960 were constructed using the 1956 ratio in Schultz's tables of value of physical plant to gross expenditures of educational institutions; the expenditure figures were taken from Department of Health, Education, and Welfare, *Health, Education,*

and Welfare Trends (1961 Edition; Washington, D.C.: U.S. Government Printing Office, 1961) pp. 53, 54, 56. The 1962 estimate was extrapolated from the estimates for 1958 and 1960.

4. *Health, Education, and Welfare Trends,* 1961 Edition, pp. 36, 39. Estimate for 1962 enrollment in institutions of higher education extrapolated.

5. *Ibid.,* pp. 48, 49. Estimate for 1962 faculty of institutions of higher education extrapolated.

6. See References 4 and 5 and U.S. Bureau of the Census, *Statistical Abstract of the U.S., 1961* (Washington, D.C.: U.S. Government Printing Office, 1961), Table 550, p. 421.

7. See Reference 3. In the construction of the 1960 estimates, ratios of net expenditures to gross expenditures in 1956 were used.

8. An estimate of earnings foregone by high school and college students in 1960 was constructed using the method of Theodore W. Schultz (see *loc. cit.,* Table 2, p. 575). Data on weekly earnings in 1960 taken from *Statistical Abstract of the U.S., 1961,* p. 219, and data on numbers of students from the same source, p. 108. 1962 estimates derived by extrapolation.

9. Aldous Huxley, "Education on the Nonverbal Level," *Daedalus,* Vol. 91, No. 2 (Spring, 1962), pp. 279–93.

10. *Ibid.,* pp. 284–85.

11. *Ibid.,* p. 288.

12. *Ibid.,* pp. 279–84.

13. *Ibid.,* p. 292.

14. *Ibid.,* p. 292.

15. Morris Kline, letter to the writer, January 12, 1962.

16. Nathan Glazer, "The Wasted Classroom," *Harper's,* Vol. 223, No. 1337 (October, 1961), p. 151.

17. Lawrence S. Kubie, "Creative Scientific Productivity," *Daedalus,* Vol. 91, No. 2, pp. 307–08.

18. Jerrold R. Zacharias, report of address before the American Physical Society and the American Association of Physics Teachers, *The New York Times,* February 23, 1961, 23:2.

19. Francis Keppel, quoted in Martin Mayer, *The Schools* (New York City: Harper and Brothers, 1961), p. 387.

20. Philip H. Coombs, "An Economist's Overview of Education" in Dexter M. Keezer, ed., *Financing Higher Education, 1960–70* (New York City: McGraw-Hill Book Company, Inc., 1959), p. 25.

21. Based on cost estimates of Theodore W. Schultz (see Reference 3), enrollment figures of U.S. Office of Education (see Reference 4), and the

estimate of Gary S. Becker that tuition amounts to about two-thirds of the total educational costs of colleges and universities. Gary S. Becker, "Underinvestment in College Education?," *American Economic Review,* Vol. L, No. 2 (May, 1960), pp. 347–48.

22. For projections of trends in costs of higher education see Seymour E. Harris, "Financing of Higher Education: Broad Issues" in Keezer, *op. cit.,* pp. 35–77.

V. THE UNITED STATES AND THE COMMON MARKET

1. *United Nations, Statistical Yearbook, 1960* (New York, [1961]) .

2. Emile Benoit, *Europe at Sixes and Sevens* (New York: Columbia University Press, 1961), p. 5. Because countries differ in the relative prices and relative quantities of the different goods they produce, close comparisons of their total national product are not possible.

3. Robert R. Bowie and Theodore Geiger, *The European Economic Community and the United States,* a study paper prepared for the Subcommittee on Foreign Economic Policy of the Joint Economic Committee, 87th Congress, 1st session (Washington, D.C.: U.S. Government Printing Office, 1961), pp. 22–25.

4. Benoit, *op. cit.,* p. 18.

5. Bowie and Geiger, *op. cit.,* Table 1-A.

6. Bowie and Geiger, pp. 22–25, and *Economic Report of the President, 1962* (Washington, D.C.: U.S. Government Printing Office, 1962), p. 210.

7. Bowie and Geiger, *loc. cit.*

8. *Ibid.,* Table 1-B.

9. Benoit, *op. cit.,* p. 116.

10. *New York Times,* January 15, 1963.

11. *Wall Street Journal,* April 24, 1963.

12. It was so described in the EEC Commission's *Sixth General Report,* issued July 1963, Part I, p. 7.

13. Press conference remarks of July 29, 1963, *New York Times,* July 30, 1963.

14. Walter S. Salant and Beatrice N. Vaccara, *Import Liberalization and Employment* (Washington, D.C.: The Brookings Institution, 1961), p. 263.

15. *Ibid.,* p. 270.

16. Alfred Marshall, *Principles of Economics* (8th ed.; London, 1920), p. 270.

17. D. H. Robertson, "The Future of International Trade," in *Essays in Monetary Theory* (London, 1940), p. 214, reprinted in the American

Economic Association's *Readings in the Theory of International Trade* (Philadelphia, 1950).

18. See Ragnar Nurkse, *Patterns of Economic Development*, Wicksell Lectures (Stockholm, 1959), 14 ff.

19. Folke Hilgerdt, *Industrialization and Foreign Trade* (Geneva: League of Nations, 1945).

The manuscript was edited by Elvin T. Gidley. The type face for the text is Linotype Baskerville, cut in 1931 by the Mergenthaler Linotype Company and based on a face originally designed by John Baskerville between 1750 and 1758. The display face is Bulmer, which is a replica of a type face originally designed by William Martin for William Bulmer about 1790.

This book is printed on Warren's Olde Style Antique White Wove paper made by the S. D. Warren Company, and bound in Fromson Orban Company's Elephant Hide Paper over boards. Manufactured in the United States of America.